PRAISE FOR
SHOTGUN ANGELS

Jay DeMarcus's story will strike a chord with everyone who reads it. I can certainly relate to many of his trials and tribulations. However, it's not where we've been but where we end up that counts. I firmly believe that my own faith has also brought me to where I am in this journey called life. I hope that when you read this book, you will be as encouraged, enlightened, and uplifted by my dear friend Jay as I have been.

Todd Chrisley, entrepreneur and
star of *Chrisley Knows Best*

When I moved to Nashville to start shooting the ABC show *Nashville,* Jay DeMarcus was one of the first artists to befriend me and make me feel welcome in the town he knew so well. Like countless others, I was already a big Rascal Flatts fan, which continues to this day. The difference is how blessed I've been since getting to know the guys—perhaps especially Jay. In Nashville, some people are said to be "a good hang"—which means that any time spent with them always seems to be time well-spent. Jay is the definition of a "a good hang." He's hilarious and heartfelt. And with such an incredible career under his belt, he's got stories that'll make you laugh, stories that'll make you cry, and a whole bunch of stories that'll make you do both. So if you're about to read this book, buckle up and get ready for a good hang and a great read!

Chip Esten, actor and singer/songwriter

$2.50

We all get asked at one time or another, "How did this happen for you?" Usually our answers are uncomfortably awful. But Jay DeMarcus has dug deep inside to look not at his career but at himself. Such a rare look inside has created a rare book. Enjoy.

Cris Collinsworth, NBC Sports broadcaster
and former NFL wide receiver

Working with Jay DeMarcus for the last decade has been a career highlight for me. His creativity and talent not only as a founding member of Rascal Flatts but also as a songwriter, a broadcaster, and a Grammy Award-winning producer touch on his many, many talents. And I'm also proud to call him my friend!

Scott Borchetta, president, CEO, and founder
of Big Machine Label Group

SHOTGUN
ANGELS

SHOTGUN ANGELS

MY STORY OF BROKEN ROADS
AND UNSHAKEABLE HOPE

JAY DEMARCUS

WITH TIMOTHY WILLARD

ZONDERVAN®

ZONDERVAN

Shotgun Angels
Copyright © 2019 by Jay DeMarcus

Requests for information should be addressed to:
Zondervan, *3900 Sparks Dr. SE, Grand Rapids, Michigan 49546*

ISBN 978-0-310-35503-8 (hardcover)

ISBN 978-0-310-35815-2 (special edition)

ISBN 978-0-310-35518-2 (audio)

ISBN 978-0-310-35505-2 (ebook)

The events and experiences detailed herein are all true and have been faithfully rendered as the author has remembered them, to the best of his ability. Some names, identities, and circumstances have been changed in order to protect the anonymity of the individuals involved.

Art direction and cover design: Curt Diepenhorst
Cover photo: Jeremy Cowart
Interior design: Kait Lamphere

Printed in the United States of America

19 20 21 22 23 24 25 /LSC/ 15 14 13 12 11 10 9 8 7 6 5 4 3 2 1

To my wife, Allison,
and our two precious babies, Madeline and Dylan

CONTENTS

Dear Reader 11

1. First Times 15
2. Coda 25
3. Deep Roots, Rich Soil 35
4. All That and a Sack of Potatoes 49
5. Good-Bye, Columbus 65
6. More Wild Turns 83
7. Scraping By 97
8. Some Beautiful Things Can Crush You 107
9. My Downward Spiral 123
10. Losing My Way 129
11. Fiddle and Steel 149
12. That's Not Going to Work for Me 165
13. Beautiful Winds the Broken Road 187
14. Eternal Sadness of a Satisfied Soul 199
15. Shotgun Angels 215

My Ultimate Hope 225

Acknowledgments 231
Notes 233

DEAR READER

First things first. You may have seen my picture on the cover of this book and thought to yourself, *Huh, I know that guy. He's in that band that sings the song my cousin got married to. Something . . . Broken, da-da-da, something. "God's Broken Road . . ."* No. Wait. Ugh. Ah! *"God Bless the Broken Road." That's it!*

So you decided to pick up a copy, and here we are, beginning our journey together. By now you might be patiently waiting for me to start "getting to the good part" and dishing on all things Rascal Flatts, but that's a story for another time. I'm sure at some point it will be told, and the three of us will do that together.

This is the story about me and my journey. The story of how a most unlikely kid from Columbus, Ohio, ended up in this crazy place. I have found myself many times, while writing this book, marveling at the stories again. Some of them seem too far-fetched, too hard to believe. But they happened. They're real. And it still blows my mind.

Of course, Gary and Joe Don are some of the most important people in my life. As such, to think they won't be mentioned here and there in this story, well, that'd be just silly.

When I think about the road that led me to where I am today,

I can't help but ask myself, "Why? Why was I the recipient of such an extraordinary life?" It's a puzzling question. I can get turned around on it if I think about it too much.

But here's the deal.

I believe we are all recipients of extraordinary lives, if we choose to live them. Ah, but therein lies the challenge, the proverbial "hard part." Sometimes getting to live out your extraordinary life takes sacrifice, patience, tenacity, some "roll up your sleeves and get your hands dirty" grit, a dash of luck sprinkled with some faith, and all of it covered with hope.

But what keeps us from choosing to roll up our sleeves, to do the work needed to reach our goals? I believe the number one thing that keeps so many of us locked into that safe and familiar place is the fear of failing.

Well, I hate to break it to you, but here's something that's not a big secret:

You are going to fail.

If you're like me, you're going to fail miserably sometimes. But how you deal with the failure—how you learn from it, how you move on, how you let it make you smarter—that's what counts. Not the failure itself.

So, are you ready? Are you ready to figure out whether you're the kind of person who will get knocked down and keep getting back up? Or will you fold like an accordion under the pressures that life is sure to bring your way? I believe you and I can choose to be one or the other.

But we need help.

We cannot do it alone.

Trust me, I know. Because I've had a lot of help. I couldn't have made it to this point without it.

I've had loved ones encourage me when I was ready to quit.

I've had pastors counsel me in my darkest days.

I've had friends send me a text or an email just to let me know they were thinking of me.

But I've also had one thing that supersedes them all, and this is that story.

Thanks for coming along for the ride.

Chapter 1

FIRST TIMES

If you want to walk on water,
you've got to get out of the boat.
JOHN ORTBERG

The show was supposed to start in thirty minutes. There was only one problem: the band couldn't make it.

I stood staring at my watch. I couldn't magically make it stop snowing. I couldn't pull a new artist out of a hat. Ron Rhoerenbeck, the venue owner, was in a bind. "I've already sold tickets," he told all the volunteers for the concert, myself among them. "The crowd expects a show."

He had no plan B. This was my only play.

I paced frantically back and forth in the back of the theatre, waiting for my roommate, Alec, to show up. I was already there working and had decided it would be better for him to grab my things and run them to me than for me to leave and come back.

"C'mon, c'mon."

This was the King's Place, a premier concert theatre in the heart of Columbus, Ohio, on a Saturday night. Tickets sold, butts in the seats, ready and eagerly waiting for a show.

I kept my eye on the door.

This is stupid, I thought. *Why did I volunteer to do this? What was I thinking? I don't even have a set list. And I've never played a real concert, not alone. And no, leading church worship services doesn't count.*

I didn't feel the cold of the Ohio winter. But the artist who was scheduled for tonight sure did. They were stuck in the snow and had to cancel.

Sure, I'll just volunteer myself as the backup artist. No problem.

I think I covered everything, I thought to myself. *The bag of cords, the sustain pedal, the stand. God, I hope Alec brings everything I need.*

The people were filing in.

And these people? What are they going to think?

Then the voice of Doubt crept in.

"Are you crazy? Do you think you can go up there and hold these people's attention? This crowd expects to see a real artist. You think you can make them want to stay and listen to you and your silly keyboard? Who are you? You're nobody."

I didn't like Doubt's tone. But too often he was persuasive.

Out of the dark snowy night my roommate emerged. He swung the car around and frantically grabbed my gear.

I lugged my keyboard from the back seat and set it on top of my stand. In minutes, I had my whole rig set up on stage behind the curtain. But I couldn't shake my anxious thoughts about the crowd of fifteen hundred people who stood milling around, wondering what was going to happen.

My heart was pounding out of my chest. My hands were cold and clammy.

What in the world was I thinking? I thought to myself again as I peeked out from behind the long, crimson velvet curtain that covered the front of the stage. I looked at all those people who were expecting someone else, and I almost froze.

Almost.

Then I closed my eyes and took a long, deep breath. I said a prayer to myself, and a sudden calm came over me. I could hear my mother's voice in my head. "Bubby, God gave you these gifts, and this is what you were made to do. You can do this."

Now, the nerves just didn't stop. They shifted into more of

an adrenaline rush. I was refocused and anxious, ready to go. I had no idea what in the world I was going to do once I got out there. It was just me, my trusty Korg M1 synthesizer, and fifteen hundred of what had to be the most confused people in the world staring back at me.

The walk to that keyboard seemed to last forever. Once I was there, I took another deep breath, put my hands on the keys, and just started to play some chords.

"Hey, everybody," I said, "I'm Jay DeMarcus. Welcome to the King's Place. Yep, I know I'm not who you came here to see," I continued, "but thanks for sticking around. Now let's see if we can't have a little fun tonight."

I played a little more, and then I began to sing. Nothing complicated, just "Our God Is an Awesome God." I heard a few voices join in and then a few more. Suddenly, the whole crowd was singing.

I'm sure I smiled to myself and breathed a sigh of relief. This wasn't hard for me. I had played in church, behind my mom, leading worship a thousand times. So I did what I knew how to do best and led them in more worship tunes: "Holy Ground," "He Is Lord," and "Our God Reigns," among others.

This probably went on for ten or fifteen minutes until I summoned up the courage to stop and speak. I explained to them that due to the weather, the scheduled act had to cancel, and Ron had asked me to step in and do a few tunes, and I was grateful and humbled to be there.

If my memory serves right, the first song I played after the introductory worship tunes was "When God Ran" by Benny Hester. I remember feeling for the first time what it was like to be up there by myself, standing there, listening to people applaud and cheer for just me. It was a strange sensation. Because up until that point, I had always performed with other people, in a band, or with other singers. I had never done anything by myself.

But I wasn't alone that night.

I could feel the gentle hand of the good Lord guiding me. I know it sounds strange—I get it. But sometimes you just know he's there.

I could also hear the words of my mother encouraging me, and my dad's voice in my head, saying, *You see, all those years you thought I was being too hard on you, not showing you anything? Well, you wouldn't have been able to do what you're doing right now, buddy.*

I welled up with tears. The moment was not lost on me. Everything that had led up to that one moment came back to me in a blur.

I turned my attention to my M1. I had just started learning how to sequence tracks on it, so I thought it'd be fun to guide the audience through a tutorial of how to program a song from the ground up. I started with a drum groove to an arrangement of the old hymn "Love Lifted Me."

I then added a bass part and some synth pads, and soon the song began to take shape.

Then I dialed up a piano patch and began to solo over my "one-man band" tracks. People clapped and cheered me on. And in the middle of it all, something occurred to me.

I was having fun!

I was in my element, right where I was supposed to be.

The nerves were long gone.

The exhilarating feeling of entertaining people, holding their attention with music that I was making, coursed through me. It was a feeling that was second to none. I was hooked.

I wrapped up my little set with "Here's My Heart" by David and the Giants. It had been a huge "accidental" pop crossover hit in the late 1980s. I quit playing on the last chorus so I could hear just the voices sing it. I stood there listening, taking in the moment, realizing how special being up there really was.

I never wanted to forget it, and I never have. Now, I'm sure some people left when they heard the artist they'd bought tickets for didn't make it. But it sure seemed like most people stayed. I remember walking off the stage that night, and Ron said, "Good job, pal. I don't know what we would've done."

I'll never forget my time volunteering at the King's Place. It holds a special place in my heart. I got to meet and see a lot of the artists I admired and, frankly, wanted to be like. That venue was a beautiful window into the heart of the Christian music industry and provided me a view of that scene I wouldn't have had otherwise.

Years later when I was in the industry myself, I would reconnect with many of those same artists, and many would remember meeting me and remember very vividly a little concert hall on Tussing Road in Reynoldsburg, Ohio.

Ron rewarded me for stepping in that night by letting me know that my band, Fair Warning—the first band I'd ever formed—could open for the "real" band, Halo, he'd recently scheduled for a concert.

Man, I loved Halo. I couldn't believe it. The night wasn't a total disaster.

All those nervous thoughts that jammed into my brain just

before I went on? They left. Well, maybe they didn't leave. Maybe they just settled down.

And maybe the voice of Doubt that rose up in me every time I let myself daydream about being a real musician morphed into another voice—a hopeful one. It's hard to let yourself hope when you're young and the fear of failure likes to play mixed martial arts and put strangleholds or armbars on your dreams of success.

But maybe that's what hope is, I thought.

What if hope is actually the movement of fear in my life—and what really separates the two is the simple act of taking a step toward doing what I love?

STEP UP OR GET LOST

Fast-forward to a random Tuesday night—Printer's Alley, Nashville, Tennessee. But this time, Gary, Preston, Shane, and I are scheduled to go on at the Fiddle and Steel.

I started to panic. I had no idea what we were going to do.

No guitar player?

We'd been packing out the joint for the past few months. Every Monday and Tuesday. And now this. Who could play on such short notice? More importantly, who would even know the songs?

Then it hit me.

I know who's available tonight.

I picked up the phone and called Joe Don Rooney, a guitar player I'd recently hired to play with me in Chely Wright's band.

"Hey, man, I need a guitar player tonight. You think you can sit in with me and Gary?"

"Yeah, man," he replied. "I'm not doing anything. I'll be there."

Great. That's covered. Now I had to break the news to Gary that Shane couldn't play because he was sick.

When I told my cousin Gary, he didn't take it so well. And why would he? He'd only been in town for a few months, and we had our "thing" going. It was familiar and good. We'd found a killer groove at this venue.

"What if he doesn't know all the songs?" Gary asked. "I mean, I don't even know him."

I understood. Those were reasonable objections.

"Man, if this sucks," continued Gary, "I'm bailing early. I'm not going to play until three in the morning with somebody I don't know and who doesn't know any of our songs."

Fair enough, I thought.

But what Gary didn't know is that Joe Don had grown up listening to the same music we'd grown up listening to. All the songs Gary and I played? Joe Don knew them all.

Gary finally agreed.

We took the stage that night. And something like magic happened. I can't really explain it. You just know it when you feel it. And we all felt it.

We haven't been apart since.

Do you see a common thread in these two snapshots? I mean, besides me panicking.

That second snapshot? That was our first night as Rascal Flatts. Well, we didn't name ourselves Rascal Flatts that night, but you get what I mean. We discovered each another. And in that moment, a lifetime of hopes and dreams, fears and failure, collided.

Was it luck? A bit, yes. And quite a bit, no.

When I think about that night at the Fiddle and Steel and about standing in the snow that Ohio night waiting for my roommate to show up with my keyboard, I don't just see luck. I see first-time moments in my life where hard work met opportunity. Those moments combined fear and hope.

Fear required me to step up or get lost, to put my ability to the test. And hope was what made me move.

Chapter 2

CODA

Can't reach the sea if you can't get past the sand.

"CHASIN' THE WIND," *CHICAGO TWENTY-ONE*

What if I told you that you're going to win a Grammy. Or that you're going to win the Super Bowl. That you're going to become the CEO of Apple. That you're going to _____.

Go ahead, fill in your dream. Probably feels insane or uncomfortable to write what your heart is really feeling. An impossibility.

Why would I write something in the blank? It's no good. It's not going to happen.

It felt insane for a skinny, scrawny, awkward, "run the wrong way in a basketball game" kid from Columbus, Ohio, too. If someone would have told me twenty years ago that I'd be where I am today, I would have laughed in their face. Maybe you would too.

And I get it. It's not easy to fill in a blank space with a dream you've already convinced yourself will never come true. For crying out loud, I flunked my driving test when I was sixteen (three times I failed it!), and I never ever won the one-hundred-meter dash at field day, and I never got to play wide receiver for the Cincinnati Bengals—I'm with you on shattered dreams and impossibilities.

"I guess it couldn't hurt," you say, as you start filling in the blank. "It's not going to happen," you say. And I'd say the same.

But dreams do start in blank spaces. They begin in the dark, standing in the snow, waiting for your roommate to not screw up your one chance. They begin when your guitar player gets sick and you're left staring impossibility in the face. They begin like a song with no words—out there, waiting to be carved into music by a willing hand.

The Grammy? The Super Bowl? The CEO job? Those are final movements. They're codas stamping a life with a cool bit of finality and purpose, right? That's what a coda is in music—a concluding section. And all these great goals and achievements? They're fantastic conclusions of the lucky, the special ones.

Or so they say.

What if I told you hope doesn't care what you do, how famous you are, how far you've fallen, or how much money you have? What if I told you hope was built along the broken road by hard work, sacrifice, disillusionment, and toil, and that those broken pieces along the way contribute to the stanzas of a heart that hopes? The cadence of an unbreakable spirit. The grit in the face of a world that says it's okay to give up, to let hope go.

What if I told you that hope can carry you when no one is around? What if I told you a heart that hopes can bring healing? What if I told you that a little bit of heaven can come into the world through you and me if we lived more recklessly in our hope?

Would you believe it?

AN IMPOSSIBLE, CONTAGIOUS FAITH

How many times have you heard a celebrity or an athlete say something like this in an interview: "Man, I've been so blessed." I'd venture to say you've heard it more often than not. At times it almost seems programmed—like it's a response given to them by a teacher in media training school.

To be fair, I've said it.

In fact, I still say it. A lot.

It's not an insincere response. I really do feel that way. But recently it occurred to me that I've never really thought about what it means. After all, it's easy to say you're blessed when things are going well—when you've aced those finals at school, thrown the winning touchdown pass in a big game, or received a raise because you presented a genius marketing plan that fired up the whole company.

Easy, right? I'm blessed.

But what about those times that aren't so rosy? When a loved one or a friend dies. When you lose your job because of downsizing. When a younger recruit comes in and steals the starting quarterback job from you.

Or when you've been in a country band for eighteen years and it becomes harder and harder to produce hits, sell tickets, and stay relevant. Not so easy then. Your pride gets hurt, and you feel like you've been kicked in the gut—passed over, forgotten, old news. We've all been there at one time or another; we've all felt that sting.

Who can still say they're blessed even when the hard times come?

This is one of the reasons I decided to tell my story. Because on the surface, there is Jay, the dude from Rascal Flatts, the "funny one." But you may be shocked to hear that I do not consider my greatest blessing to be Rascal Flatts. When I look back over my life growing up and my early career and consider all the things that happened along the way that shaped me, I'm reminded of how miraculous this journey we call life really is.

The journey was and still is a blessing. And it's not been all bright and shiny either. Life has sometimes flat-out sucked. And at times, the sucking has gone on for years on end. At least that's the way it felt. And yet those moments made me who I am today. Man, I know it sounds weird, but that's a blessing.

You know, it's easy to get sucked in to thinking, *Man, if I can just get some more money or more status or move into a bigger house, then I'll have arrived.* That's the blessed life, right? But when we live always looking down the road, wishing for another life, we miss the most beautiful parts of life right here, right now.

Now don't get me wrong, Rascal Flatts has been and continues to be a wonderful blessing, to be sure. It's something I could never have imagined in a million years. But my greatest? Not even close.

Now, I know what you're thinking: *Oh, he's gonna say his family, duh!*

Yes, they are a great blessing too, no doubt. But my greatest? Nope.

My life's greatest blessing is hope.

It may seem oversimplified, but hope is powerful. Think about it.

Hope gives us the drive and the determination to keep going, to never give up. Sure, I could list a million things here—my wife, my mom, my kids, my dad—all great blessings without a doubt.

But the one thing that has been a constant source of strength, a pipeline to peace, a life vest in a sea of sadness and disappointment, is hope.

Sometimes hope feels like a precious commodity; it's not easy to come by, and yes, there have been times when I've felt like I used up all my hope.

But just when I felt like my "hope tank" was going to be empty, all my fuel was going to be depleted, something would happen—a phone call from Mom, an encouraging word from a friend, a quote on a church's marquee sign, a song on the radio—just a few ounces of hope sprinkled here and there, just enough to keep me going. It was always there, just in the nick of time.

My story is improbable, bordering on the impossible, if you look at it from a simple human, practical point of view. In many ways, I'm a textbook example of the American Dream. I come from humble beginnings, raised mostly by a single mother who worked two jobs and struggled to make ends meet. We lived in a small house in a not-so-great neighborhood. We wore hand-me-down clothes, and forget about my mom ever having a new car—she drove very used cars, like the 1978 Ford Thunderbird with more than 200,000 miles, with plywood covering the floorboards where they had rusted through.

I'm not complaining because we never felt it; we never felt like we didn't have much. We always had enough to eat. Those two jobs sent us to private Christian schools. Christmases always seemed magical. And my sister, Tiffany, and I always felt loved. But the biggest thing from my childhood that stands out to me is that we were always in church, and I mean always. Ugh.

Church twice on Sunday.

Church on Wednesday night.

Choir practice on Tuesday.

Any time the doors were open, we were there.

Through a kid's eyes like mine, sometimes it seemed a bit excessive, I will admit. And growing up in a Pentecostal church, watching people shout, run down the aisles, and jump in the pews, it also scared the crap out of me on more than one occasion. But even though I was a kid, it was not lost on me that there was a reason my mother was able to have so much on her plate and not completely lose her mind.

You see, she lived from paycheck to paycheck. The extra holiday shifts she picked up at Kmart were to ensure that our Christmases were magical. I knew it. I watched it, and I marveled at it. I also knew how she did it.

My mom had hope.

This isn't the point where I start cramming Christianity down your throats. This isn't the point where I turn into a Bible-thumping browbeater. I'd never presume to preach to someone. But I am a believer.

I could go on here with a story about how "my faith has pulled me through," but I have something more—I have evidence.

Evidence that my mom's faithfulness paid off. All of it—her dragging us off to church, sometimes against our will and sometimes when she was too tired to stand, dropping her last bit of change into the offering plate without knowing when she'd have more. It paid off because God, her Father, her Savior, never failed her.

He never let her down.

I watched for it, thinking there would surely be a time when her faith was shaken. It was not. Her foundation was strong; her foundation was her faith, and her faith gave life to and fueled her hope. And it was contagious.

I couldn't help but be inspired by it. I started to believe in the impossible. I started to believe in miracles because I was living in them.

People often ask me when the moment was that I gave my life to Christ and became a believer. This may sound strange, but for me, it was never a choice. I had to believe in God, because he has proven himself to be real too many times in my life.

So I have to start with hope.

Everything for me begins with hope.

I can count a multitude of blessings, but I have to say that even my obstacles, even the dark times, are blessings. Strange thing to say, I know. But those were the times when I had to dig the deepest, when I've had to tap into that hope, even if it was elusive.

I'm going to tell you some things that you won't believe. I'm going to share stories with you that, even while I type them out, I still find hard to believe myself.

This book isn't meant to pat myself on the back. It's simply to share with you the journey that I've been on—the twists, the turns, the broken roads that have brought me to this place. Because if God can use someone like me, if he'll do these things for a kid from Columbus, Ohio, who sometimes had no clue where to even start, he will do them for you.

So take a leap with me. Just consider there's someone or something higher than yourself out there; someone who loves you, believes in you and only wants the best for you. Let's start with that basic premise. Then we can go from there. Take a shot. What do you have to lose?

Chapter 3

DEEP ROOTS, RICH SOIL

A gift, though small, is welcome.

HOMER

My mother's name is Caron (pronounced Karen) Eileen Kirk. She's from a little place in West Virginia called Dunlow. It's one of those "blink and you'll miss it" kinds of towns. I've been there a few times, and it's beautiful—old-timey railroad beds surrounded by mountain views, complete with a rolling creek, straight out of a Norman Rockwell painting. She grew up there—a hundred-acre chicken farm—with her brother, my uncle Jimi, and her parents.

Mom loves to describe the West Virginia farm as a picturesque place, and I can see why. Well, I can mostly see why.

They lived an isolated mountain life in their own little corner of the world. The farm had a simple, rustic kind of beauty. It had a big barn and a chicken coop. And even though it spanned a hundred acres, they only tilled half of it. They grew everything they needed to eat. Money was tight, so they lived off the land.

They also had eleven apple trees, some peach trees, raspberry bushes, blackberry bushes, and blueberry bushes. They even grew a pawpaw tree in the front yard. If you don't know what a pawpaw tree is, join the club. I had to look it up after talking to my mom about the farm. It's a popular tree in the Southeast because of the edible fruit and because it looks tropical.

They used an outhouse—they actually had two of them, and they thought they were the rich people. For those of you reading this who never watched *Little House on the Prairie*, an outhouse is where you go to the bathroom, and it's not actually in your house—thus, "*out*house." No plumbing, so you don't flush anything—think Porta Potti for your home. It looks like a tall, narrow shed. I'm thinking about building one behind my house in Nashville. I wonder what my wife, Allison, will think about it.

Mom likes to tell me about how unique the house was.

"It had doors everywhere," she says. "Four doors in the front and the back, and two doors on each side."

That's a lot of doors.

She says unique, I say weird, but I'm not going to debate her on it. It also had two fireplaces and a well. Now, the well was on the back porch, which was actually a unique place for a well. Mom says they used to drop a large bucket into the water and pull it back up with a chain. Once the bucket was up, they'd use a dipper, or what you and I might call a ladle, and drink right from it.

What strikes me about Mom's farm life is that she explains it as being nothing but a time of joy and beauty.

"The farm was surrounded by three mountains," she says, reminiscing. "I could see a mountain from each side of the house except the back. And in the winter when the snow would come, we'd play with the icicles, using them as noses for our snowmen, or we'd just suck on them."

They also had a horse named Bill. You know, because it's such a common name for a horse. Mom and her brother, Jimi, were too small to use Bill for plowing, so their mom would sit the two of them on the tiller and strap them down with the leather tiller straps, while she directed ole Bill as he pulled it up and down the rows.

No John Deere here, my friend.

They tilled the ground with a plow and Bill.

In the winter, Faye, my grandmother, whom I called Mammaw (pronounced Ma-Maw), put my mom and Jimi to bed in the living room where the fireplace was. To help keep them warm, Mammaw would hold up a towel in front of the fireplace and then wrap their feet with it. Mammaw took care of the farm and did the heavy lifting at home.

Jim, my grandfather, was a coal miner. Tough job. He'd been one since he was twelve years old to help provide for his family during the Great Depression. For years, Jim, whom I called Pappaw (pronounced Pa-Paw), worked every day in the mines of West Virginia with his dad. But when the mines shut down, he had to learn a new trade. That's when my uncle Mack came into the picture. When he and my aunt would visit my grandparents, he'd talk to Pappaw about finding new work because all the mines were closing.

Uncle Mack told Pappaw about glazing. So Pappaw learned how to be a glazier. No, it's not putting glaze on donuts! It's the trade of installing windows, storefronts, doors, and mirrors—all glass, all the time.

But to learn the trade, Pappaw had to travel back and forth from the farm in West Virginia to Columbus, Ohio. He'd come home to the farm from Saturday to Sunday afternoon and then return to Uncle Larry's house in Columbus to keep learning the glass-glazing trade. Eventually, in an attempt to provide a better life for his family, Pappaw packed up Uncle Jimi and my momma and moved them to Columbus. My mom was thirteen.

I like to think those West Virginia mountains shaped my mom's tenderness, while the bare-essential living instilled in her an intuition that kept our household feeling like we had plenty, even though we had next to nothing.

HAMMER-N-NAILS AND LITTLE BIRDIE

My mother's entire side of the family was quite musical; my pappaw was in love with bluegrass. He had his own band that played in local beer joints—they even won a couple of local "battle of the bluegrass bands" contests. He played a mean Dobro and banjo, not to mention a "flat top" acoustic. Mammaw also sang and played.

But it was Pappaw who gave me my earliest musical training.

Pappaw and I had our routine. He'd pick me up after school on Friday afternoon. We'd grab a Rofini's pizza on the way. After devouring the pizza, Pappaw and I would sit out on the front porch. He'd give me a guitar and show me some chords. And as I banged them out on Mammaw's old Gibson Dove acoustic guitar—which was sunburst-colored, with a special pickguard— he'd play along on his Dobro. It was my earliest education in the world of music, and I loved every minute of it. My mom gave me that guitar for Christmas three years ago, and it's the very one on the cover of this book.

Pappaw listened to the Grand Ole Opry every Saturday night. As he began to teach me how to play the guitar and these old country tunes, I got a fast education in all things bluegrass. From Ralph Stanley and the Clinch Mountain Boys, to Bill Monroe and the Bluegrass Boys, to Roy Acuff, to Bashful Brother Oswald, who played Dobro, and, of course, his favorite banjo picker, Stringbean. I knew all these names—musicians who were members of the Grand Ole Opry—at a very young age because Pappaw had followed them so closely and loved their music. I got ribbed a lot in school early on because it wasn't typical for a kid living in Columbus, Ohio, to be so well-informed about bluegrass music. At the time, I didn't see the oddity, but now I kinda get it. Perhaps I would've made fun of me too.

Needless to say, it was a surprise to a lot of people when I was growing up that I had such a deep knowledge of bluegrass. But Pappaw was an accomplished musician. He could really pick. He could play any song—he knew what he was doing. I was only a kid, but I started to pick up bits and pieces. He was very patient with me. He'd take his time and really show me how to play.

"Little Birdie" was the first song he taught me—I think they call it the clawhammer—on the banjo. On that song, you don't actually pick with the banjo picks; you just kind of strum it like Grandpa Jones did.

"Keep on the Sunny Side of Life" was the first song he taught me on the Dobro.

After Pappaw and I finished our little jam session on the porch, we'd go inside and join Mammaw and watch *The Dukes of Hazzard* and *The Incredible Hulk* and, if I was lucky, a little bit of *Dallas*. But *Dallas* was the "for adults only" show, and when it did come on, Mammaw sent me straight to bed. As a result, I never found out who shot J. R—kidding, of course!

If my parents wanted to punish me, all they had to do was say, "Well, I guess you're not going over to Pappaw's house this Friday." And I straightened right up.

I loved spending time with Pappaw like that. He taught me so much, including how to build things. He taught me how to use tools—every tool known to mankind. And I mean that. Every one of them. He drilled me on every tool he had in his toolbox. He'd open his toolbox and pull out the tools one by one.

"What's this?" he'd say.

"Flathead."

What's this?"

"Phillips-head."

"What's this?"

"A T-bevel."

"And this?"

"Allen wrench . . . Vise grip . . ."

On and on we went. I knew them all.

Over time, Pappaw accumulated three small houses that he used as rental properties. So he was constantly keeping them up, remodeling them, fixing stuff. I'd follow him around and watch what he did. I became really good at a young age at using my hands and building things—using saws, hammers, levels, squares, and screwdrivers. I knew more than the typical boy my age would have known, that's for sure.

I remember we once stopped by one of the booths at the Ohio State Fair. The name of the game was "see if you can drive a nail straight into the board," and if you could, you'd win a stuffed animal. I stood there and looked at all these bent nails in the wood. It seems that nobody could drive a ten-penny nail straight into a two-by-four.

"Young man," said the man behind the booth, "you wanna try that?"

"Yeah," I replied. "I can do it."

I drove that ten-penny nail straight into the two-by-four. (It's the small victories!)

"Well, I'll be," he said, somewhat surprised that I'd done it. "You'd be amazed at how many folks—and I mean adults—can't drive one nail into a board."

I still have this old picture of me and Pappaw standing side by side, hammers in hand, driving a piece of plywood up on a wall. I wanted to be just like Pappaw. I copied everything he did. If he wore a glasses pouch in his shirt pocket, so did I—even if it was huge and didn't fit into my little pocket.

One of my greatest childhood memories is sitting around at my grandparents' house listening to the entire family sing together. I didn't realize how special it was at the time, but thank God that Mammaw had her old Realistic cassette recorder rolling for most of those singalong sessions. I still have a few of the cassettes, and whenever I'm feeling particularly melancholy or just lonesome for them, I put the headphones on, push Play, and take a trip back in time. It's amazing how hearing the sound of their voices transports me right back to that room.

You know, hope is one of those rearview-mirror things. You don't realize it's being sewn into your life until later on when you look back. You adjust the mirror so you can see a little better, and there it is.

Pappaw holding my hand on the hammer just so.

Or nodding his head as I clawhammered that banjo, smiling from ear to ear.

Seeds of love watered with time.

It's only when you look back on those moments that you see how important they were, and still are. Sometimes we have to look back to see hope in full bloom.

I'm adjusting my mirror now. And I'm seeing that those times with Pappaw were cultivating the hope inside me that I would so desperately cling to later on in life.

Don't you love to look at your rearview mirror sometimes and recognize the moments that are life-changing and the gratitude we feel because of them? We could all probably do a little more of that.

CHURCH AND BEER JOINTS

My dad's family was a different story. My father's name is Stanley Wayne DeMarcus; he was the second youngest of four boys and two girls. I never knew my grandparents on his side, but by all accounts, his mother, Gladys, was as close to a saint as anyone could possibly be. It always sounded as though she needed to be in order to put up with my dad's father, Ira Lee.

Ira Lee was a hard man who had grown up being abused both physically and verbally, and he passed this on to my dad and his siblings. Ira Lee had a tough time, to say the least. He battled alcoholism and walked out on his family when my dad was a very young man.

Even though my dad's childhood was tough, one thing he and his brothers had in common was their love of music: bluegrass, country, gospel—you name it, they loved it. They played together in church, beer joints—anywhere anyone would have them.

Then when my dad was thirteen years old, he and his brothers were hired to play on a radio show. My dad was hooked. Music was going to be his life.

He would quit school when he was a sophomore to play music full-time, pursuing his dream of "hitting the big time." He would move to Sydney, Ohio, as a teenager, close to Columbus where the gigs and the money were better.

My dad was an incredible musician. He played anything he put his hands on and had the purest, prettiest tenor voice. I marveled at his ability. He was mostly self-taught and played by ear, and those ears were golden.

As fate would have it, both families ended up in Columbus in the early 1960s. Given that both my dad and my uncle Jimi made their living playing in clubs, eventually their paths crossed. Jimi needed a piano player in his band, and since my dad played piano and left-hand bass, he fit the bill perfectly and they didn't have to hire a bass player—icing on top of an already delicious cake!

So it was. They were a perfect pair.

FALLING IN LOVE, GIVING UP DREAMS

They played all over the place. Musical brothers, compadres in the trenches together. They were great entertainers. I know this because I have a recording of them from 1968, recorded in a small bar in Chillicothe, Ohio—two years before my dad would meet my mom.

One fateful day, my uncle Jimi took my dad to his parents' house. That was the day he met my momma. My dad will tell you he was immediately smitten. My mom, being young and naive, thought he was nice but didn't think much more about it until one day my dad called her up and asked her to go to a country music festival with him. My mom reluctantly agreed, but she was still unsure, as my dad was seven years her senior. But I guess she had a better time at the festival than she bargained for. Persistence won the day, and my dad was finally able to win her over.

They began to date, and from the outside it seemed perfect.

Both of them were wonderful singers and musicians. My mom was doing her own thing with a local act called "Phil Beasley and the Mohegan Ramblers." Phil tried to sing, but it was clear to everyone that Mom was the star.

Eventually in 1969, my mom would be convinced to enter Ohio's Country Music Queen contest. Phil and his band would back her. She won the title by singing Tammy Wynette's "Stand by Your Man."

First place!

My mom was going to be a star!

First prize included opening for Loretta Lynn and a Decca Records recording contract.

But it was not to be.

My father was not happy at all. He saw this as him losing her to Nashville and ultimately to stardom—a stardom he himself craved. I'm not saying my dad was jealous, but for a talented, proud man who was trying to do the same thing himself, it had to have been a tough pill to swallow.

So he presented my mom with an ultimatum. He said it was either him and their relationship or the record deal. She couldn't have both. And so it would be. My mom would pass up the opportunity of a lifetime—the opportunity to live out her dreams.

Over the years, I've asked my mom if she ever regretted making that decision, to which she always replies, "I wouldn't change a thing, Bubby (yes, my mom calls me Bubby), because I wouldn't have had the privilege of being a mommy to you and Sissy" (yes, she calls my sister, Tiffany, Sissy).

So Caron Eileen Kirk and Stanley Wayne DeMarcus would start to build a life together, and on August 22, 1970, they were married.

Not long after that, on April 26, 1971, a little boy came into the world and into their lives. They would name him names he would never be called by, leading to all kinds of confusion later in life when it came time for him to get his driver's license, open bank accounts, enroll in college, print wedding invitations—you name it. It would be an interesting and quite confusing ride.

They would name him Stanley Wayne DeMarcus Jr. But those around him would call him Jay, short for Junior. For months, no one knew what to call me. My dad wanted a namesake, and that was the only reason I could come up with for picking these names.

Don't worry, I'm as confused by this as anyone. The problem was that neither he nor my mom liked either Stanley or Wayne. Go figure!

I guess for a long time, I didn't totally understand my momma's decision to hang up her dreams. To be honest, it hurts me a little bit to think about her doing that for my dad. But I'm a father now, and her reason for doing so strikes a chord with me. And it challenges me. Would I have the same strength to make that decision for my family?

My mom and dad stand in my life like strong characters in a great novel. The novel is my life. And its plot is shaped by the deep West Virginia roots of my mother and the honky-tonk grit of my father's passion for music. But like all good stories, the hope found in the innocent beginnings doesn't always last. A storm of some kind enters the pages and makes hope feel lost and forgotten.

Chapter 4

ALL THAT AND A SACK OF POTATOES

*The truth is that it is not the sins of
the fathers that descend unto the third
generation, but the sorrows of the mothers.*

MARILYN FRENCH

Mom could do anything with a potato.

Fried? You got it.

Mashed? No problem.

Boiled with asparagus? Well, let's not get carried away.

I remember that sack of potatoes leaning against the wall in the kitchen when I was young. Potatoes were cheap. You could buy them in bulk. And she could use them for everything. Potatoes were the duct tape of the kitchen, a fix-everything catchall.

She'd cook up potatoes and mix in onions and hotdogs or sausage. She'd bake potatoes, slice potatoes, fry potatoes, skin potatoes. She'd make cheesy potatoes, potatoes au gratin. Mom was a potato superhero.

But it wasn't just Mom's potato wizardry that made her special. She was a spiritual rock. And I needed a spiritual rock because our family life wasn't all that and a sack of potatoes. See what I did there?

I mean, we had our moments—our good moments, our loving moments, our fun moments. But I guess some moments carry more weight than others.

A SHOTGUN, A SALVATION, A DEPRESSION

We lived at 144 Clinton Street. It was a small two-story townhome. Mom told me that the first song I started to hum along with was the theme song from *Green Acres*. I was only three years old at the time. Mom will tell you she knew then that I was going to be musical. That little house was where I formed my earliest memories of childhood. I remember that house well because it was right down the road from Mammaw and Pappaw. They lived at 113 Clinton Street.

My earliest years, we could walk down to Mammaw and Pappaw's house anytime we wanted. I remember we spent a couple Christmases in that house on Clinton Street.

But then we moved up north. Mom and Dad purchased their first real home—a rancher—up in Westerville. My dad stayed in that home all his life until recently.

At that time, Dad was still playing music in bars, eking out a living as a musician. But the pressures to provide a better, more consistent living mounted—that, and the fact that he'd been unfaithful to my mom a couple times. As you can imagine, that was a tough mixture for my mom, and it led to them separating and then finally getting a divorce. I was about seven years old, maybe a bit younger.

Anytime a husband and wife separate, people get hurt. After all, separation and divorce by their very definition are "a breaking," a severing of relationships. And not just any relationship. Not just a friendship. But a marriage relationship. It's the joining of two lives, and in many marriages, kids are involved. I was one of those kids. And that "complete" feeling of a mom and dad being around, of caring for you? That ended. And when you're seven, that's confusing. And at seven, you're old enough to hurt.

When my parents separated for the first time, Mom, my sister, and I moved in with Mammaw and Pappaw back on Clinton Street. The Clinton Street neighborhood wasn't a great neighborhood.

The small homes were close together, with the yards hemmed in with the old-fashioned chain-linked fences.

One afternoon, I was outside playing in the yard, and as my mom reminds me, my dad pulled up in his car, picked me up, and put me in his car. The next thing I know, I'm with Dad at our house in Westerville. I don't remember too much about the episode, but I do remember that Dad was agitated and frustrated. And that was a new thing to see in my dad.

Typically, my mom and dad did their best to hide all the interpersonal stuff they had going on. They didn't argue or fight much in front of me and my sister, Tiffany. At least, we never saw or heard them verbally fight. I never saw my dad upset. But when he took me back to his house, I saw Dad uncovered.

He was visibly upset. And he was upset at Mom.

I guess he thought that by taking me, he could somehow punish her for taking me and Tiffany away from him, for not talking to him, for leaving him.

Then things got really weird.

Dad loaded his shotgun and placed it by the front door.

"If anyone tries to come take you away, I'll shoot 'em," he told me.

In that instant, my dad became a stranger to me. I didn't know who this man was. I didn't know this angry and confused man.

Who was this man who put a loaded gun by the door? I thought.

It scared me. I remember how tense everything felt between me and my dad, and between my mom and him, during this brief span of days. It was tough.

But as my mom recalls, after a few days of being alone with me and being a full-time dad, he realized that taking me probably wasn't the best idea in the world. I think he suddenly realized he was going to have to actually be a parent with me there every second. So after a few days, he called my mom and said, "You need to come get this boy."

Mom came and picked me up and took me back home to Mammaw and Pappaw's house. It was good to be back—safe and sound. The ordeal spilled out of me back in my room as I cried into my pillow. They weren't tears of fear; they were tears of sadness—the bitter-tasting kind of sadness, the sadness you don't want to feel when you're a kid. I was sad because my family was broken apart. And I also felt bad for my dad because I could tell he was going through a lot of pain, and he didn't know how to process it.

You know, one definition of hope reads "grounds for believing that something good may happen."[1] When the pieces of your family lie strewn on your bedroom floor when you're seven years old, grounds for believing that something good may happen are scarce. Some may even say a situation like that is *hopeless*. But isn't it interesting how the human heart constantly yearns for the good in this life? Isn't it kind of beautiful that you and I automatically want reconciliation when things break in relationships? I know that when we become adults, bitterness can too easily set in, and that youthful desire for the good in all things can flicker, like a candle in the wind.

But when we're kids, there's something in us, something untainted, untouched by the adult world that pushes toward the good in things. It's almost as if the only grounds we need to believe that something good will happen are the broken pieces. Like a puzzle, we want to put the pieces back together. We want to mend. Why can't adults just pick up those pieces and complete the puzzle?

Well, sometimes they do.

About a year after the separation and divorce, Dad called Mom and told her that he had found Jesus and had begun to attend church. He invited her to go to church with him. And Mom went. And kept going with him.

Finally, along with everyone else who knew my dad, she noticed a change in him. It was real, tangible. You could see it in his eyes. He was a changed man. Kinder, more loving, more patient—to everyone. I remember he would sit at the piano and sing "Pray for Me" and "The First Million Years," and the tears would just flow. This change moved my mom, and she decided to remarry him and try to put our family back together.

I suppose I was too young to remember all that happened between Mom and Dad during this time of healing and restoration. But it restored in me that feeling of trust that I'd had, and loved having, in our family. That feeling of trust? That's hope too. You and I can be sources of hope for each other. And we can do that by giving each other a reason to trust.

So we moved back up to the house in Westerville. And for nearly seven years, things were good—they were really good. Dad took a "real" job with Columbus Janitor as an account manager for the churches in central Ohio selling janitor supplies.

And though this new job got Dad out of the bars, it also took him away from the thing he loved doing more than anything— music. Dad wasn't your tie-and-coat kind of guy. I think this kind of lifestyle eventually weighed on him and started to chip away at his soul. For someone who had all this music in him, it probably felt like a part of him was dying. I'm sure he dealt with depression for having to get up every morning and sell janitor supplies to people. That kind of work didn't satisfy him.

Here was a man who possessed all kinds of gifts for music, only to be relegated to using those gifts to play praise and worship music on Sunday mornings. Of course, I'm not suggesting that playing in the worship band is bad or ungratifying. What I'm saying is that someone like my dad, someone who possessed an obvious gift for music, wasn't made to only use this gift on a Sunday morning. He needed more outlets, especially since he'd lived his life and raised his family for a time as a musician.

I think sometimes we make things too cut-and-dried in our world of work. How many times have you heard someone talk about "real" work or a "real" job. That kind of talk can confuse young people and even adults. It can inadvertently force them into thinking they need to shelve their aspirations of pursuing a career that may not be what most folks consider to be the norm.

I'll be the first to tell you that making it in the world of music is tough, and it requires great sacrifice. But that doesn't mean it shouldn't be pursued. It may be idealistic to think it, but I wish we'd broaden our scope of what a "real" job means. Of course, I say all of this, and yet my son Dylan, who is six, still asks me when I'm going to get a real job.

In a lot of ways, I think my dad felt stuck; he didn't have a way out from where he was in this "real world" life. As a result, slowly but surely, Mom and Dad's relationship started to deteriorate again. And I think it was largely due to Dad's personal battles with work and feeling depressed about where he was in life. He became angry again and became verbally abusive to all of us.

By this time, I was about fourteen years old. I remember one incident in particular during this time. The two of them got into another argument in front of the house. Mom began to walk away from Dad, refusing to engage in a shouting match with him.

She started to walk into the house. But when my dad saw her walk away, he said, "Fine, we'll drive somewhere else so we can talk."

"I'm not going," replied Mom.

I saw my dad pick up my mom and throw her in the passenger seat so they could have their conversation somewhere else. That was hard to watch.

On another occasion, after we'd moved out again, Dad drove over to our place, wanting to talk to Mom, and he was out front waiting, but she wouldn't go outside and speak with him. So I was the one who had to go out in the front yard and tell him.

"Mom doesn't want to speak to you; you need to leave," I said.

I could see the hurt in his face and the tears welling up in his eyes. It killed me to have to be the one to tell him that and cause him pain. It sucked. There I was, a teenager, stuck in the middle of it all.

My parents' second divorce followed soon after.

Knowing my dad now, he's the kind of man who will reflect on those moments with a soft heart. He'll tear up, ashamed that those moments happened—that I saw certain events unfold. I know Dad had it tough growing up. I said it before—his home life was rough. His past haunted him and caused him to seesaw between his calloused and rough upbringing and his sincere love for his own family. Our pasts can be difficult to overcome, especially when they're carved into us with such coarseness.

Thankfully, Pappaw owned the three houses on Clinton Street. He let Mom, my sister, and me stay in one of those houses after the divorce. And it was in those following years as a teenager that I followed closely and even clung to Mom's faith. I watched from the shadows as her faith kept her strong for me and Tiffany and how it continued to give her hope.

MY MOM'S SUPERPOWER

I realized I had a young mother, and in some ways, we grew up together. Mom's faithfulness inspired me to have my own relationship with Christ. My love for Mom moved me to be a support to her and not a hindrance to her. That was important to me.

Our greatest power together in our relationship? We could always talk about anything. Still do!

And I will be forever grateful for my mom's ability to talk with me at anytime, anywhere, about anything. I could be honest with her about absolutely anything—and I mean everything. She supported me, no matter what. And I knew it.

I was raised to wait until marriage to have sex. It's kind of a big deal in the church—the infamous sin of fornication. But as fate would have it, I lost my virginity when I was seventeen. And the first thing I did was burst into my mom's room in the middle of the night and sob by her bed. The guilt and the anguish were so crippling.

I told her what I had done. And she listened. And she gave me firm words of wisdom. I felt like I'd screwed up so badly, but she was right there for me. She didn't throw judgment at me. She knew I felt horrible. She was just there.

Man, that is one lesson I hope to carry on with my own children. To be able to be there for them in their time of need. To be there to laugh with them in their times of joy and share tears with them in their sadness. That's a priceless commodity.

It took a special person to be my mom. To deal with a kid who only ever cared about music. Maybe she knew this, deep down somewhere, when she gave up her own music dreams for me and my sister. We weren't even around then, but I wonder if she somehow knew she possessed that power—to be our mom, to make life feel full no matter what, to shower us with love, to listen to us spill our guts, to believe in our dreams, even as hers lay on a shelf in the pantry somewhere.

ANGELS IN THE GAS TANK

When I was eight, I attended church camp. I wanted to come home because I wasn't in a cabin with my friends. (I was only eight—c'mon, cut me some slack.)

Mom will tell you that she didn't have a dime to her name. But she knew she had to pick up her little boy at church camp, even though the camp was in the middle of nowhere and she had no money for gas. All she had was a two-dollar gold piece that the church had passed out to commemorate the new church building. I don't even know what a two-dollar gold piece is; all I know is that's all she had. But that wasn't stopping her from coming to get me.

When she got on the road, she quickly pulled over to a gas station to look at a map because she didn't know how to get there. She discovered the camp was ninety-three miles—one way! When I talk to her about it today, I can hear the excitement and wonder in her voice.

"And all I had was that gold piece, Bubby, and barely any gas!" she says. "I laid my hands on the dashboard and prayed. I said, 'Lord, I have to go pick up my boy. I'm not doing anything here, Lord, but picking up my boy. Help me get him.'"

Not only did she not have much gas, but the gas gauge was broken. So Mom had no idea when she'd run out. She just kept driving. The gas station attendant asked her if she wanted some gas. When Mom gave him the gold piece, he said, "That's not a lot of gas, ma'am." But he did it. He put in two dollars' worth.

Mom drove 186 miles on two dollars' worth of gas to pick me up. And when I jumped in the car, she asked me if I had any of the money left she'd given me for the week. She'd given me five dollars in five envelopes, five dollars for each day to use to buy something at the camp store. Mom didn't have gas in her car, but she made darn sure her little boy had money to spend at the camp store. See? Superpower.

But wouldn't you know it, I had torn the envelopes open and used the money and bought a T-shirt with it. Mom was hoping I'd come back with a couple envelopes left so she could get gas for the ride home. Nope. But it didn't matter. We made it back home safe and sound.

Mom returned to work the next day. When she was done with work, she walked out to find the two back tires flatter than a pancake.

"I went in and called Slim and told him about the two tires," she recalls. Slim was Pappaw's friend who ran the local gas station. He came over to my mom's work and said, "It's a good thing you didn't have a long trip yesterday."

"But I did, Slim. I drove 186 miles to get my boy."

"Well, someone was watching over you. Some flat-tire angels or something."

"Slim, his name is Jesus."

My mom loves this story, and so do I. She tells me, "Bubby, I drove 186 miles with a two-dollar gold piece and two flat tires. It was Jesus. He's the love of my life; he comes first."

He sure does. But I like to think I'm a close second.

CENTERFOLD LOVE

My mom had some crazy superpowers. And she was a believer in Jesus. And I mean a real believer. You don't drive nearly two hundred miles with no gas and nearly flat tires without the Holy Spirit in your corner. And she had him and trusted he'd get her to where she needed to go.

But as wonderful as my mom's faith was, she was no pushover. She was smart and firm, and nothing got by her.

How many idiotic things do we do as teenagers? Stupid things we never forget. Dumbass things we regret.

I worked at my grandfather's glass company during the summer of my senior year of high school. A bunch of the men who worked there would bring in *Playboy* magazines, and when they finished with them, like an idiot, I'd take them home and hide them under my bed between the mattress and the box springs.

Well, one morning I walked down the hall to take a shower. We had one bathroom in the house, so my sister, my mom, and I had to share a bathroom. When I was in the shower that morning, my mom—who mysteriously knew where I had hidden the *Playboys* (actually, she found them one day when she was cleaning my room)—took the centerfolds from every single magazine I had hidden and taped them to the walls of the hallway.

When I opened the door, my sister was standing at her door—her bedroom was the first room to the right as you walk out of the bathroom. She stood there pointing her finger, laughing at me.

I stepped into the hallway, mortified.

Thoughts jumped all around in my head.

What had I done?

I felt ashamed and embarrassed.

But it wasn't like I was fifteen. I was getting ready to graduate. I was eighteen. I was an adult. I could do what I wanted now. Right?

As I walked down the hallway, I slowly peeled off the centerfolds one by one, dripping wet in my towel, listening to the cackle of my sister. My room was opposite the bathroom at the end of the hall. It felt like the longest hallway ever. Mom's room was the last door on the right, next to my room.

I stopped in front of her room, holding the crinkled-up centerfolds in my hands. Mom's door was open. She just stood at her vanity, slowly brushing her hair. When she saw me, she turned to me in an easy kind of way that made me feel even worse.

She stepped toward me. She took her hairbrush and smacked me hard, twice, on my wet right arm. It stung like fire.

Then she looked at me with an intensity I'll not soon forget—as if she was about to drive her words into my brain with a hammer.

"Don't you ever disrespect this house with that filth again! Do you understand me?"

She had an uncanny ability to humiliate the urination of a dog out of you.

My mom never wavered in her principles. The times I remember best remind me of how her firm yet gracious and deep love for me forged its way into my heart and made me a man.

DAD DID NOTHING FOR ME, AND EVERYTHING

I started playing piano around the age of ten. And yes, I took some lessons. But lessons—learning to read sheet music? That was not all there was to learning how to play music. Music comes from somewhere inside of you. It's expressed through singing, through playing instruments.

And whether you play music or not, nearly everyone feels music deep within them. It's a visceral and almost magical art form. But in our house, this art form came from hearing.

Do you remember the song "Hard to Say I'm Sorry" by Chicago? Of course you do. I loved that song. And my dad loved it too. I loved the musicality of it. I was hooked on the arrangement. When I listened to that song, I knew then that music was all I was ever going to want to do.

One day, I asked Dad to teach me how to play that song. His reply surprised me.

See, Dad taught me chords on the piano. We had this old upright Wurlitzer piano that I'd bang on after Dad showed me some chords. When I heard that Chicago song, I tried to play it. But I couldn't figure it out.

"Dad, can you teach me to play this song by Chicago?"

"Listen to the song," he said. "Then play what you hear."

Thanks for nothing, Dad.

"But can't you just show me how?"

"Listen to the song, Jay."

Dad pushed me to play by ear. He knew that by pushing me to really listen and figure it out on the piano by myself, it would expose my desire to really learn how to play the piano. Did I really possess the desire to see it through?

Well, I listened and tried, and then listened some more. But I finally figured out how to play that song. It's hard to explain the feeling of accomplishment I had when I'd done it. When I told Dad I had learned it, he just smiled and winked at me. Sure, he could have showed me how to play the song. But for Dad, learning comes from your desire to really get into the music—to listen to it and have it become a part of you.

The best thing my dad did for me was not show me one thing. And in doing so, he showed me everything.

I guess I shouldn't say he didn't show me anything; he showed me some scales and basic chord structures, and then he threw me headfirst into those musical waters to see whether I'd sink or swim.

When I learned that song, I felt like a Jedi Padawan who'd learned how to use his first tool of the Force. I wasn't sitting at the piano playing chords; I was constructing my first light saber. I was young Skywalker who'd learned his first lesson from Yoda. It would have been cool to find a Wookiee somewhere—or a Princess—but being a Jedi was cool enough.

Chapter 5

GOOD-BYE, COLUMBUS

*Opportunity is missed by most people because
it is dressed in overalls and looks like work.*

ANONYMOUS

1991—a year of change. That was the year, if you recall, that rock music shifted away from the hair band, hyperstylized scene of 1980s metal toward the grunge era. If you can't remember because you weren't born yet, let me refresh your memory just a bit.

Bands like Nirvana, Pearl Jam, and Soundgarden took over in the rock world. It was a time when the feel-good party music and lifestyle of the '80s gave way to the melancholy of skepticism. The mood of the youth in our country turned to angst.

So we had a country full of angsty young adults who loved flannel, ripped jeans, and combat boots. Now, I'm not going to deny that if you look on YouTube, you may or may not find old footage of me on the Christian music festival circuit sporting a flannel around my waist. Perhaps some cut-off jeans? Maybe boots? I'm not sure. You'll have to check. Grunge was indeed far-reaching.

Nirvana's "Smells Like Teen Spirit" became the anthem of a generation, along with Pearl Jam's "Even Flow." The riff-driven tunes and dramatic crooning took over, and eventually they filtered into the Christian music scene. I remember the Christian music group DC Talk releasing their *Jesus Freak* album in late 1995 to wide acclaim and massive sales. It wasn't hard to hear the grunge influence on the title track "Jesus Freak."

Now, I'm sure you're wondering, why is a country musician talking about grunge music? Simple. It was a year of change.

A year of change in the world of music, one that was felt widely. I'd argue that even country music felt the massive shift. It was also a year of change for me.

But you know, change doesn't announce itself. It just sweeps up on you, like waves on the shoreline. And when the waves recede, the sand looks much different.

WHO AM I NOW?

Do you remember the Isuzu I-Mark? An iconic vehicle. Four doors of sheer sleekness, capabilities rarely found in a midsize sedan. Sure, now you remember it, right?

Well, if you can't quite place the iconic I-Mark, just know that this incredible vehicle was mine—all mine. It was my first car. And I didn't just drive it; I wore it like an old shirt. A teenager's first car is his castle—okay, well, actually it was my third car. I also owed about $2,200 on it. So at nineteen, I had a car payment. Life was underway. Now I was a real adult. I had debt.

There wasn't anything too special to write home about in my life. I lived in an apartment. And I was playing piano in church, leading worship music with my mom. We both served as the music minister. We split the time and the salary.

It was just enough of a gig to whet my appetite for a life in music. Ever since my dad taught me to play Chicago, I wanted to venture down the road that led to becoming a professional musician. I was consumed with practicing. The hard lesson Dad taught me about listening to music and figuring out how to play it took root deep inside me. Now my love for music could grow with the developing ability to play anything I set my mind to.

But who was I? Just a kid leading worship with his mom in a forgettable town. I had no idea how to get started on the road to becoming a professional musician. I discovered that when you don't know how to get to where you want to go, the best thing to do is be where you are. Dig deep. Work hard. And work extra hard on what you believe God has called you to do in this world. And how do you know that? By the feeling in your gut. I knew when I learned Chicago that I wanted to keep learning like that. I knew that's what satisfied me.

I think sometimes we complicate God's purpose in our lives by making it a mysterious thing we have to figure out. But we don't have to figure it out; we just need to pay attention. It's funny because when we're kids, we naturally gravitate toward doing what we love. We listen to that inner voice that tells us, *Yeah, this is cool—do this!* And we do it over and over again.

When we grow up, we tend to mystify things. Everything gets so serious and adult-ish that we fail to listen to our inner voice. You get that first mortgage payment, utilities, car payments, soccer practices, dance recitals, and my personal favorite—colonoscopies (here I come screaming toward you, fifty!). In short, you get more responsibilities. I suppose I was still young enough to have some of that *Man, I want to wake up every day and play and perform music!* in me and continued to listen to the voice pulling me down the path.

But all I knew how to do was play. I didn't know anything about becoming a professional musician. Sometimes, however, that's all you need to know. You just need to know how to work at something—hard and consistently hard. Though hard work is no guarantee of making it as a professional anything, it's a step in the right direction.

I also learned that you need to put yourself in the center of things. If you want to be a farmer, you're not going to live in New York City. If you want to be a race car driver you're going to want to hang out at the track. Watch, learn, get behind the wheel and race, crash, and win. So, I practiced, found a small music hub in my hometown, and got involved.

I found a core group of friends who had similar interests and tastes in music, and we began to play. Some of it wasn't very good at first, but it was enough to give us a taste and keep us going. We played whenever and wherever we had a chance to. And more than anything else, it was just fun.

Elliott Allison had just gotten out of the Air Force and moved back to Columbus and had begun attending my church. He was a few years older than me and a great singer.

We became fast friends and spent a lot of time playing music. Elliott and I would make music together for years to come; he'd be in every incarnation of a band I had during those years. In those days, we sang it all. Everything from the Paynes and the Imperials to Whiteheart, Allies, and Petra—southern gospel to rock and roll.

GIVING YOU FAIR WARNING

Remember when I was pacing outside the doors of the King's Place waiting for my roommate to return with my keyboard setup? Well, the King's Place was my hub. It was a Christian music venue east of Columbus, Ohio, in Reynoldsburg, just off Route 70—right down the street from the Motorcycle Hall of Fame.

I loved going to the King's Place on the weekends. All the

Christian bands I loved came through there. I'd watch the shows and hang out and talk to the musicians. I talked to bands after the show and met anyone who'd take the time to chat with me about music.

Everybody who was anybody in the contemporary Christian music played at the King's Place—Guardian, Whiteheart (no, not White Lion), Petra, Liaison, Idle Cure, and a band called David and the Giants. Their lead singer was a guy named David Huff. When I was seventeen, I met David and slipped him one of our band's cassette tapes. We called ourselves Fair Warning, and I wrote the songs.

"Thanks," he said, being nicer than he really needed to be. "I'll listen to it."

Of course, my brain was exploding. David Huff was going to listen to my songs. A total big deal. David's band had written a hit song that ended up on WNCI 97.9 by accident—the big pop station in Columbus. One of the DJs accidentally played the very overtly Christian song "Here's My Heart." The phone lines blew up. People loved it. It became a huge crossover hit, and they rode the wave of that single. It meant so much to me, a seventeen-year-old, to keep in touch with David.

So much of this world is built around relationships. Don't ever underestimate the power of a good relationship. There are plenty of people out there who attend events to push themselves, to network, to self-promote. You'll always have those kinds of people. But if you take the time and spend the energy to build relationships, the real reward is found in meaningful connection.

And I don't mean with "getting in" either. I mean, even if you don't make it or get in, the reward for building relationships is the relationship itself. That's the beauty of connecting with other human beings. Life looks like one gigantic puzzle, each piece a person connecting to another connecting to another to make a beautiful picture. It's particularly true in the music world. The saying "it's who you know" is true—but not in the sense that just networking and getting to know people will qualify you; rather, in the sense that when you establish relationships, gain trust, and develop a reputation for your work ethic and talent, then people will connect you to other people and projects.

I remember the story of David from the Bible. Before he was King David, he was a musician, and his reputation went before him. When the king needed a musician to play soothing music to help calm him in the evenings, one of his staff recommended David because he was a skilled player. No self-promotion for David. He just played for his sheep under the stars. I didn't play for sheep, but I did keep working at my craft. And I did do my best to establish relationships.

What's so cool now is that I'm still in touch with a bunch of the musicians from the King's Place. One such person wound up being my A&R director at Benson Records years later—Bill Baumgart, who was there traveling and playing keys with the band Liaison. It is indeed a small world, especially when you see people as people and not simply a means to an end.

This connection with David was my first blip on the radar. A confidence booster. A nugget of hope.

Some weeks later, the phone rang.

"Bubby, phone's for you. Someone named David," said Mom.

I ran downstairs. No, I flew. It was David from David and the

Giants, and he wanted to talk about my cassette. Our phone was in the middle of our kitchen, which happened to be the place where the whole family congregated. I could barely hear the voice on the other line. So whenever we needed to create some privacy for a conversation, we'd take the puke-green handset with the squiggly cord and stretch it as far as it would go—over by the basement steps—and shut the door on the cord behind us (we went through a lot of cords).

"I like your stuff, Jay," he said. "There's good writing here, and the vocals are great."

I couldn't believe he'd taken the time to pick up the phone and call me. I told him I'd love him to produce some stuff for us. We chatted a little more and then hung up. It was the first time a real musician recognized my ability. He told me he'd like to stay in touch, and we did. Now, I'm sure this was just a blip on David's radar screen, and he may not even remember it to this day. But for me, it was everything.

That's the kind of unintentional impact you can have on someone's life without even knowing it. In those moments, David taught me the value of taking the time to be kind to someone while expecting nothing in return. He didn't know me from Adam, but he took a few moments to give a kid, a fan of his band, a little bit of hope, some fuel for the tank.

You never know who you're going to connect with. But the point is to do your best to connect, period. I'm a professional musician now, but I'm also a husband and a father. And connecting with people continues to mark my life in the deepest of ways. I don't ever regret making a new friend, and I love going deep with my closest friends.

Relationships matter not just as professionals but as family members, community members, and citizens. Sometimes I think we forget how important other human beings are. We get so wrapped up in ourselves and our cell phones and our social media—and I'm definitely guilty of that too!—that we get into a transactional mode as people; we use people instead of love them. But it's a surefire way to get off track.

WHAT'S A CHAPERONE?

What was my future?

I'd always intended to go work for my grandfather's glass company and install windows and eventually run that company. However, he had to sell it when Mammaw's health took a turn for the worst and he needed to be home with her.

So that kind of put a dent in those plans, but that was my post–high school plan—that, and to keep playing music. I had no intention of attending college. I couldn't afford it.

But that all changed one day when my pastor asked me to chaperone a youth conference in Indianapolis.

"Jay, we need someone else to go with the youth pastor because too many kids are going to the conference. He needs some help. Would you be interested in going along as a chaperone?"

A chaperone? I was nineteen at the time. Barely out of high school myself.

This youth conference was massive. Thousands of kids attended, all from youth groups representing Midwest churches. There was a full lineup of guest speakers, guest musicians, and bands. Lee University had their group there as well—New Harvest—which was led by a guy named Danny Murray. Danny taught at the school and traveled with this group of student musicians. They'd play at events like this, representing the school. The musicians in New Harvest represented the best of the best from Lee. Danny picked them, and most of them had been given various scholarships for music.

Of course, I knew none of this about Danny and the group prior to the conference. I barely knew what a chaperone was. But my youth pastor had told me he was in a bind. I liked him, so I decided to help out. And I'm pretty sure I had nothing else better to do that weekend, truth be told.

Danny's group played a worship set on Friday night and blew me away. The vocals, the musicianship—everything was spot-on. I heard they were from Lee University, but even for college students it was a level of professionalism I'd rarely seen. After the session ended, I made my way down to the front of the stage and found one of the kids who'd been singing, Javen Campbell.

"Hey, man," I said, "you guys sounded great."

He bent down and talked to me for a few minutes.

"Thanks," he replied. "I'm Javen. Nice to meet you. What are you up to?"

"Thanks—I'm Jay. I'm here as a chaperone with my youth group from Columbus, Ohio."

"Oh, great. What do you do there? Are you the youth pastor?"

"No," I replied, "I'm just helping out."

"That's great. Do you play music?" he asked.

"Yeah, I do. I play piano at my church. My mom and I co-lead the worship—she's the music minister and I play for her."

"Wow, that's fantastic! Are you in school?"

"No, I'm not."

"Hold on a second," he said. "Hey, Danny," he yelled across

the stage. An older guy turned around. (I say "older," but he was probably only in his early thirties. When you're nineteen, anyone over twenty-five looks old.) I could tell Danny was the leader of the group.

"Come over here a minute," said Javen.

So Danny walked over and knelt next to Javen.

"Danny, this guy's name is Jay. He plays piano for church with his mom."

As this encounter was unfolding, I remember feeling very strange about it. Not in a bad way. But it was bizarre that these two people gave me the time of day and seemed genuinely interested in me.

In my mind I was thinking, *Well, this is weird. I just wanted to tell them they did a good job and move on.*

But then Danny said, "So you play piano? Do you read music?"

"Well," I said, "I play by ear. My dad taught me how to play, but he really forced me to play by ear."

"The student who used to play keyboards for us just graduated this weekend. The guy playing for us this weekend is just filling in. Are you in school?"

Again, the same question Javen had asked me—and again the same answer.

"No, I'm not in school. I've got a job, and I help out at the church with my mom as a music minister."

He looked at me quizzically and said, "Why don't you meet me here Sunday morning at eight o'clock before the service starts?"

I didn't know this guy from a stranger on a street corner. The whole encounter felt so otherworldly to me at that moment. I guess sometimes you can just tell that God's up to something. I didn't know how to respond.

"Here, as in right here?" I asked, clearly stalling.

"Yeah, just come on up on the stage—just be here at eight."

We parted ways, and I don't remember exactly what I said or if I gestured that I'd be there or what. But Saturday rolled around, and I was still mulling over my chance meeting with Javen and Danny.

And I honestly didn't know if I should meet Danny at eight o'clock the next morning. I suppose the old voice of Doubt started to creep in again; he's a persistent bugger. And there were still so many unknowns about Danny and his intentions, which made me naturally apprehensive. But after arguing with myself, and with Doubt, for most of Saturday, I said to myself, *What the heck. Who knows what's going to happen.*

Sunday showed up right on schedule. And so did I—8 a.m. on the stage. Danny asked me a few questions—just small talk. Again, the question about being in school; he asked what church I attended back home in Columbus.

"Langley Church of God."

"Oh, so you're a Church of God boy."

"Yeah, I grew up Church of God."

He again told me they were a group from Lee University.

Then he asked me to sit down at the piano—the piano that was on the stage. And I did.

"I'm just going to sing some worship choruses," he said. "You follow me."

So Danny started to sing, and I started to play behind him. I suppose I was lucky because he was singing all the songs I grew up singing and playing in my church. I kept playing behind him as he sang.

After a few minutes, he stopped, turned around, and looked at me. I stopped playing.

"Do you want to go to school?" he asked.

"What are you talking about?" I replied.

"I can get you a scholarship to Lee University. But you have to be there next week."

Scholarship? Financial help? School?

Attend Lee University?

Next week!

What the—

I stumbled over my words and said, "Uh, I don't know, Danny. I just met you. And I have to work next week. I've got bills, a car payment. I just don't know how I'd do something like that."

I've got bills?

A car payment?

I guess I was excited, but it didn't seem real. It all seemed like it was going by in slow motion. And at any instant I could wake up. I guess I didn't have any answers for him; I only had excuses.

He looked at me and said, "Get your expenses together and what you owe and send them to me. I'll call you Monday morning. But I'll need an answer."

I walked away from the morning meeting like a zombie.

I couldn't believe all that had happened to me inside of forty-eight hours. But I got in my car and made the two-and-a-half-hour drive back to Columbus, sat down with my mom, and told her the story.

She sat there and bawled her eyes out. She was beside herself with a good sadness and a good bit of joy.

"Mom, Danny said he was going to call Monday morning. If he doesn't call, we're going to know it was all one big joke."

Mom was quiet.

At nine o'clock on Monday morning, Danny called the house

just like he said he would. I answered the phone. "Hey, Jay," he said, "can you give me a rough estimate on what you owe?"

"Okay. I have two credit cards totaling $1,800 and my car payment, which is $116 per month—and I owe $2,200 on it."

"Okay, Jay, listen," he said. "We can help you with your bills, and we'll give you a scholarship to study music if you want to go to school."

I about passed out. This was no joke.

"But I need you down here because enrollment is closing," he continued. "And we need to get started. What I need you to know is what you'll be getting into. You're going to be around some of the best students in our music program, and if you're up for the challenge, I'd love for you to come play keyboards for us and tour with us to recruit for the school. Now what that means is you won't get summers off like most other students do because we travel. We perform at summer camps, youth festivals, and camp meetings. That's how you keep your scholarship."

I was stunned. But I had to respond.

"Danny, wow, this is a lot. And it's a lot because I'd have to quit my job—you've got to give me a couple days."

"I'll give you two days, but I need your answer."

The next day I drove in to work and quit.

I forfeited my lease on my apartment, which I shared with my roommate anyway.

I got rid of a bunch of junk I didn't need.

I loaded up my Isuzu I-Mark and drove to Cleveland, Tennessee. I lived at Danny's place in his spare bedroom for the first six months because the dorms were full.

But it's not as if leaving home was just a passing thought.

I was scared, nervous, and sad—not for me, but for my mom.

Because I knew how much it was killing her that I was going to leave. She knew at that point in time—and she'll tell me this to this day—that once I left there, I was never coming back.

"I knew," she once told me, "that you were gone forever. I knew that God had bigger plans for you." What a woman!

For the next few years, I toured with Danny Murray and his group, and I recruited for Lee University. Danny and I became close friends and have remained so ever since. He was in my wedding and is still my mentor and one of my best friends. He became a second father to me.

To this day, if I have any huge decision to make in my life or if something happens in life and I'm not sure how to react to it, I'll call him and say, "Hey, I need to talk through something with you." And we talk. His family means the world to me.

I'd say that Danny, during those early years especially, helped shape who I am today. He pushed me. He was hard on me, and I'm grateful for that—of course, I wasn't at the time, but now I can see just how important it is to surround yourself with people who aren't afraid to push you, tell it like it is, and challenge you to be better. He challenged me to look at every angle of every situation and figure out the best way to address it. He operated in many ways like a field general; he'd walk into a situation and figure out the best way to tactically face it. And I loved that about him—and I still do.

I've asked Danny about that day in Indianapolis—how he knew to offer me what he did. He tells me, "There was something in your eyes I could see that was special and hungry, and something I knew I had to get to the bottom of. I knew I had to see what you were all about."

At my rehearsal dinner, he stood up and said, "Jay was always one of those people who when I first met him in Indianapolis, I could tell there was something in him—some spark in him, some fight in him. I could tell that if I threw him in the middle of a junk pile, he was going to find a way to come out driving something."

That's one of the coolest, most humbling things anyone has ever said to me or about me. Sometimes the most uncommon relationships can emerge from the most common experiences. I've learned that we just need to pay attention.

I spent three years at Lee, but I never graduated. And not for the reasons you might think.

I quit college early because I got my first record deal.

The music world shifted in 1991. And so did mine. I stepped into the super unknown. Yes, I realize that's a sneaky reference to Soundgarden's fourth studio album released in 1994. And yes, it was on purpose, mostly as a way to foreshadow (see track 3!). Foreshadowing aside, Lee University was not on my radar. And yes, it was more fuel for the old hope tank.

But even more than ounces of fuel, the experience taught me something about hope. Hope is deeply related to faith. They're cousins. We know hope is grounds for believing that something may happen. Faith is the certainty that this something is going to happen. I was hopeful I might get an opportunity someday to play music in a professional way. But I had no idea how that could happen.

When the opportunity presented itself, when the rubber hit the road—would my faith match my hope? Time would tell.

Chapter 6

MORE WILD TURNS

Success makes life easier.
It doesn't make living easier.
BRUCE SPRINGSTEEN

Call for Jay!"

While I was in school at Lee University, I had played the piano during "Lee Day" for Michael English, one of the most popular and bestselling Christian solo artists at the time. It was a family event where people from all over could visit, and we'd give them a big show and sort of "show off" the college and its many talented students. As fate would have it, Neal and I were selected to drive Michael and another popular singer at the time, Mike Eldred, back to the airport in Chattanooga.

I'm sure I was a little over the top with my enthusiasm about what I wanted to do once I left college, but they were patient and listened intently. I told them I was a songwriter and that I wanted to produce. They couldn't have been nicer. In fact, they gave me the names and contacts of some publishers in Nashville. I told Michael that once I got out, I'd love to reconnect and maybe even play for him someday.

I should've been a fortune teller. Remember, relationships matter. And meeting Michael that day was another one of those opportunities that when it presents itself, you have to jump in and not be a jerk, and care about people. As it turns out, Michael knew this bit of wisdom, and I was the recipient of his good graces.

So, based on Michael's and Mike's recommendations, I sent my demo tapes to various outlets, trying to get a deal as a writer. One day, the dorm phone rang. In those days, dorm rooms didn't have phones to the outside world. Outside-world calls came to the hall pay phone. Yep.

You know, pay phones—those odd-looking rectangular metal boxes that used to hang on concrete walls. The kind you see in old movies. They held a hard, plastic object called a receiver. You put one end up to your ear, and the other to your mouth. And if it rang, it meant a phone call was coming in. We called those contraptions "pay phones." Because if you wanted to make a call to the outside world, you inserted coins—like quarters, dimes, and nickels.

I grabbed the receiver. It was a guy named Don Koch. I had sent Don and Benson Records one of my tapes. Don was an award-winning record producer responsible for the success of 4Him; he was a hit songwriter and well respected in the Christian music community.

Don says to me, "Hey, we love your band. What are you guys called?"

"Oh, well, we're not a band. I'm trying to be a songwriter."

"Oh," he says. "Well, we like your sound. Who's singing?"

"That's my roommate, Neal."

Neal had already graduated and was working in the president's recruiting office for the university, and we were both traveling with Danny. He was two years older than me, but we became fast friends, with similar tastes in music, and we developed a very strong bond. He was like an older brother to me, and we're still close to this day. I love him dearly.

We had scraped together some money and gone to Lookout Mountain Studios in Atlanta. We recorded some of the tunes I had written, and we called the project *Destiny*. Creative, huh? We even did a cheesy photo shoot. We weren't deliberately trying to be a real act by any means at that time. I was still in school; Neal was an awesome singer; and he sang my songs the way I wanted to hear them. That's really all it was, or so we thought.

"Well, we love what you guys are doing," Don says. "Let's talk some more. Why don't you go talk to your buddy and see if you guys want to be a band for real, because we want to sign you guys to a record deal."

So I met Neal for lunch the same day.

"You're never going to believe this," I said, "but Don Koch loves our demo tape. He wants to sign us to a deal."

"What?"

"Yeah," I continued, "they want to sign us." We just sat there in total disbelief, even as we were talking about it. "Well, Neal, do you want to do this? Do you want to be a band?"

I'll never forget this conversation. There we were, sitting in a restaurant. Neal was sitting across from me wearing a tie and a dress coat. Getting signed to a record deal was the furthest thing from his mind. And to be honest, it was the same for me. I was trying to get signed as a songwriter, not necessarily as an artist. The moment hung on us like an awkward Christmas sweater that's too big but feels nice.

Neal looked at me and thought for a moment.

"I mean, I guess. Why wouldn't we? Let's try it."

It was almost more of a question than a statement.

And soon many more questions would follow.

HAVING HOPE INCLUDES DECISION MAKING

I had about a year left of school when I got the call from Don Koch. The call presented me with a dilemma. *I'm so close to finishing. Do I stay and close out my college degree? Or do I peek behind this recording contract door.* For nearly three years, I'd worked with Danny and his group. I fell in love with working in the studio and was happy. Problem was, I wasn't a very good student.

Before I met Javen and Danny, college had never crossed my mind. I had my job at the church with Mom, and I could take over the glazing business at some point down the road. That's what I saw when I was nineteen. College wasn't in the cards. I certainly never dreamed of receiving a music scholarship to enroll in one.

Now the call from Don.

You can reflect all you want on the merits of a college education. And I won't argue. College was a privilege. It gave me more than I ever dreamed it would, and I did in fact learn a lot. But if I've learned anything over my short time on this earth, it's that God's plans for his children take all kinds of twists and turns. Sure, we need to seek wisdom and good counsel when we face big decisions in life. But we should never forget that his ways are not our ways.[1]

And the truth is, sometimes we won't understand certain events or situations until years down the line. And that's okay. Well, I suppose I should say it should be okay. We like to know what's going on, don't we? We like that sense of control we feel—or think we feel—over our life.

Looking back now, I can see how this moment of decision factored into the trajectory of my life and career. It's impossible to see that perspective when you're in it. All you can do is pray, seek out the counsel of trusted friends who love you, and boldly take the next step.

I asked Danny what he thought I should do—finish school or take the deal. Danny had become one of my closest friends. I trusted him.

Danny looked at me and said, "You can always go back to school, Jay."

And that was that. Or was it?

NOT EVERYTHING WE THOUGHT IT WAS

Neal and I drove to Nashville to meet with Don Koch. We sat in his office, and he said, "I'd like to record some songs with you guys."

He slid an envelope toward us with a piece of paper in it. The figure $17,500 was written on it. But that's not how much he was giving us. That's how much it was going to cost us to record some songs with them. They were offering us a development contract, not the real deal—the big record deal you always hear about. Neal and I didn't know what to think. How in the world were we going to come up with that kind of money?

Neal and I became great friends with Vanessa and Heather Conn, the two daughters of Dr. Paul Conn, the then and current president of Lee University. So, we had a unique relationship with Dr. Conn in that we considered him a friend. As it turned out, Neal worked for Dr. Conn's office as a recruiter, so it gave us the opportunity to visit with him frequently.

Dr. Conn had gotten word of our visit to Nashville and asked us how it went. We told him about the opportunity to sign a development deal with Benson, but that it would cost us more than $17,000. Dr. Conn listened intently and was truly excited about the opportunity. But he didn't offer any advice.

The next day, Neal called me to tell me that Dr. Conn had called and wanted to see us. So we went back to his office. Once seated, Dr. Conn slid an envelope across the table with a check for $17,500 in it. I know you might be thinking, *What's with all the sliding envelopes and mysterious amounts of money?* Well, that's how it happened. Honest.

After Dr. Conn slid the envelope across the desk, he looked

at us and said, "Make us proud. I know you guys are going to do great things."

Are you kidding me?

It was more fuel for my tank. One decision leads to another, then to a string of events that stack up and show us how God is walking ahead of us, leaving nuggets of hope along the way. But in life, we don't always take the time to look around and take notice of how everything connects, of how God leads. I've learned that if you want to find encouragement along life's path, it's good to look back regularly. Take a moment to write down your path from where you started to where you are now. When you start connecting the dots, the events and meetings, the decisions and blessings, reveal the invisible hand guiding us along the way.

That day, Neal and I called Don Koch and told him we had the money. And so we finally got to work.

But you know, we never even spent all the money Dr. Conn gave us. When we were recording in the studio, the director of A&R for Benson Records, Andy Ivey, came down to the studio to hear what we were doing. When Andy heard the tracks, he said, "Stop right now. Come upstairs; I want to talk to you guys."

It was one wild turn after another.

Once upstairs, we sat at Andy's desk. And wouldn't you know it, he slid an envelope across the desk. No, I'm kidding. No more envelopes!

Andy said, "We want you to finish these three songs and then finish the record. We want to sign you to a record deal."

And just like that, East to West was born—finally, for real.

Well, it wasn't "just like that" because Neal and I had a disastrous name, Destiny. We quickly realized that nine out of ten bands use the name Destiny when they're starting out. We knew we needed something else. After a few months of searching for a name, Don Koch came up with the idea—East to West, which he pulled from the Scripture that reads, "As far as the east is from the west, so far has he removed our transgressions from us."[2]

"Welcome to the Next Level" was our first single off our debut record, self-titled *East to West*, which released in 1993. It was a wild ride for the next four years. We found success early. "Welcome to the Next Level" topped out at number three on Christian radio charts. Three more songs on that record also did well. "Heart on the Line" hit number sixteen on the charts; "Hungry for You" hit number three; and "Prince of Peace" was our first number one radio hit.

We released *North of the Sky* in 1995, and that record did well too. We toured nationally on our own and also with the big Christian pop artists Al Denson and 4Him, and we did some dates with the hugely successful group Point of Grace. We played all the major Christian summer festivals; the touring was relentless. But in some ways, my work at Lee had prepared me for that.

During that time period, we were nominated for many awards, received some critical acclaim, and were part of the wonderful pop movement going on in Contemporary Christian Music. During this time, Don was also instrumental in pushing me to be a better writer. Until that time, I'd never really cowritten with anyone. He taught me the value of collaborating with other artists.

My world, which only a few years earlier had consisted of playing music in my church with Mom, had exploded. I was literally living my dream. It's all a bit of a blur to me now, but looking back, I realize how much I was able to do in a short amount of time—from just playing with my mom on Sunday morning and the occasional concert with Fair Warning to living out every dream I'd ever had sitting on my basement steps talking to David Huff. I was living the ultimate end-game dream, or so I thought.

Neal and I had great chemistry onstage together. We had performed so long with Danny that it became second nature. We were a great complement to each other. It was fun, and it was easy. Looking back now, I don't think I realized how special those years were to me. You can never replace those first moments when dreams, not fully realized, begin to crystalize before your very eyes.

But if there's one thing I've learned these years since, it's that success brings blessing, but it doesn't make you immune to hurt. In fact, success can often be the cause of pain.

My world took a drastic turn, and I won't lie—I was excited and thankful. And maybe I was naive enough to think it'd last forever. That's what I wanted. In our dreams we don't bargain for disappointment. It just shows up. It doesn't wave a flag of warning. It comes—often with broadsiding force.

LOSING MY CLAWHAMMER

I remember that year, not only because of the release of our first record and single, but because it was a bittersweet year. It was the year I lost Pappaw.

I was still at Lee University and playing with Danny and the group during the whole "getting signed" event. And we worked hard. Danny rarely gave us breaks to go home and see family, mostly because we traveled so much while performing. But when the breaks came, we took advantage.

I remember one break in particular.

I drove home from Cleveland, Tennessee, to Pappaw's house in Columbus. And yes, I drove the I-Mark. To this day, if I can steal some time to go home, I do it. But that's harder to do now with a family. But when I was in college, that was my first thought: *Go home, see my family.* So I drove home to see him.

He and I had been through so much together. When Dad went through that rough patch years prior, it was Pappaw who stepped in to fill that void while my dad figured things out. Pappaw was a blessing from God in my life. He made such a deep impact on my life.

But he was getting older. I took advantage of the break, and I stopped in on him for a bit. After visiting with him for what seemed the briefest of times, I hugged him good-bye and turned to walk to my car.

For some reason, as I was walking away, I stopped in my tracks, turned around, and hugged him again. I pulled him tighter this time—held him closer.

I don't know how many more times I'll be able to do this, I thought to myself.

I wanted the moment to last.

That was the last time I saw him standing.

A few weeks later, when we were recording the album, my sister flew to Nashville to visit because she wanted to hang out for a bit while we recorded. I was staying at the La Quinta on Metrocenter Boulevard in Nashville.

We were headed back to the studio, but before we left the hotel, I said, "I need to call Pappaw. I haven't talked with him in a few days." Pappaw and I kept in touch all the time. It was not uncommon for me to call him once a week. So I ducked back into the hotel room and used the phone to call him. Remember, this was the pre-iPhone era. I was too poor to have one of those massive car phones you'd keep in a briefcase. I did have a pager though.

"Hey, Jay," he said.

"Hey, Pappaw," I responded. "How are you?"

"I'm doing fine, just fine. Tired is all. I just took a new job as a night security guard."

I was surprised he'd take that job. He suffered from Parkinson's disease and remained in constant pain.

"You feeling okay, Pappaw?"

"I'm not feeling too well today," he said.

"You should stay home and rest, Pappaw."

"Oh, I'll be all right."

"Okay, I'll talk to you in the morning. I love you, Pappaw."

"Oh, yeah, buddy. Lord God I love you too," he said, and then we hung up.

That night on the way home from work, Pappaw had a heart attack while he was driving and crashed. The cops found him in his banged-up car along the road and took him to the hospital.

As soon as I got word, I flew in to see him for the last time.

I sat beside him in his hospital room. He opened his eyes a couple times. And if I leaned in really close to his ear and whispered to him, he'd open his eyes and squeeze my hand. I don't know if it was just muscles twitching or reflexes. I like to think it was some sort of response. I'll never know.

I hold those moments in my heart. Me whispering to him, him squeezing my hand with his Dobro-playing hands. Those same hands that taught me to clawhammer the banjo. Those gentle but strong hands that worked so hard all his life and came alive when he played bluegrass. Those hands that steadied mine on the hammer. Those same hands that held the plywood for me so I could nail it up straight and true were the hands that held mine, guiding me through those early years of life, shaping me into a man.

When Pappaw slipped away and out of my life, it was one of the saddest moments I've ever known. He was like a rock to me. He always seemed indestructible. Seeing him there, attached to a machine in the hospital, rattled me. And losing him was the first time I really stood face-to-face with our mortality, and it shook me to the core.

I sang "I Thought He Walked on Water" by Randy Travis at the funeral. Gary was there, long before we were Rascal Flatts. He's often said to me that he doesn't know how I made it through the song, given how close Pappaw and I were. It was tough, no doubt about it. I blocked out the emotion as a testament to the impact he'd had on my life. I did think he walked on water. That song embodied everything I'd ever felt about him, and it was my tribute to him.

My bond with Pappaw has taught me more about life the older I get. He taught me the trade of glazing at the glass company, and the importance of working hard. He was one of the first male role models who impacted me; he loved me, and I knew it. Never doubted it.

We all need time to search and find our own way, but we also need people in our lives who show up when the world seems to have walked away. That was Pappaw for me.

He died in 1993 at the age of seventy.

The pain subsides, but the missing never goes away.

Chapter 7

SCRAPING BY

No one ever told me that grief felt so like fear.

C. S. LEWIS

Losing someone you love sucks. It feels like a gut punch. You fall to the ground, breathless, wheezing. For a moment you feel like you might die. You struggle to breathe, and then finally, slowly, painfully, the air somehow finds its way into your lungs. Eventually you breathe again. But not without a good bit of pain.

But if there's one thing my dad taught me growing up, it's that when you get punched, you stand up and you punch right back. You bloody some noses. And you get on with things.

I remember one winter day from my childhood when I headed outside to skate around on the ice. We lived in a cul-de-sac in Westerville, Ohio. Whenever it got really cold, the end of the "court" froze over and we'd have a nice little man-made frozen ice rink. The neighborhood kids would play on the ice—hockey or something.

I was the first one on the ice that day. But eventually, I was joined by three older boys. I guess they thought they'd have some fun with me; they were always messing with me. We were in the same Cub Scout troop together, but they were a couple years older than me. Our den mothers would take us out to the ice and let us play, largely unobserved, in lieu of a proper Scout meeting.

That day, wherever I had decided to skate around, they moved over to my patch and claimed it.

"This is our patch. Go find another place to play."

I did. I mean, I was only nine or ten years old.

They'd follow me over. And the same thing happened.

"Hey, kid, go find your own patch, this is ours."

And then it got real. The big kid pushed me. I slipped and fell down on the ice. Everywhere I went, they continued to follow me and harass me.

That was it.

I stood up and punched him square in the nose. It was like punching a water balloon filled with red syrup. His nose exploded all over his face and jacket.

It was on.

The other two boys grabbed me and held me by my coat. Meanwhile, the bloodied buffoon went to work on my gut—punching me over and over again. But I began wriggling out of my coat and eventually broke free, leaving the two kids holding my winter jacket. I ran home.

When I arrived home, I ran into my room. My dad was in the living room and wondered why in the world I came running into the house like that. Well, Dad quickly figured it out. He went outside, found the kids holding my jacket, and brought them over to the house. He had me come outside.

"Are these the kids who took your jacket?"

"Yes."

"What happened to this kid with the bloody nose?"

"He pushed me down, so I punched him."

"Well, you don't let bullies take your coat. Now I want you to fight each one of these kids and get back your coat."

Dad always was a bit unorthodox in his confrontational management. There was no getting out of this, so I went to work. And I fought each one of those kids to get my coat back.

The neighborhood parents caught wind of it, and many of them questioned if this was the best way to resolve the issue. My dad didn't waver.

Everyone finally went back home, and I walked back into the house to get warm, winter coat in hand, chin held high.

I've learned that life feels a lot like slippery ice. It's fun to play on, and it's kind of magical. But it's no fun when a bully pushes you down on the cold surface. It's also no fun when it's three against one.

Getting gut-punched over and over feels a little bit like you've been forgotten. You get enough punches, and it could be lights out.

I've experienced the loss of dear family members and friends. And I realize that life goes on. I realize that you have to just somehow make it through. But no one really sees the course of pain another person goes through. I remember talking to a friend who told me about a conversation he had with someone who had just lost their nephew. Seeing young people die has to be the worst kind of pain.

"You know, there's really no way to describe it. You attend the funeral; you say good-bye to your sister; and you drive home. My life picks up where it left off. My sister's life? A living hell."

How many people in this world make their breakfast, get ready for work, and head out on their commute, all the while living in hell? All the while doing everything they can to hold it together? How many people stand daily between two metaphorical bullies, just taking it to the gut over and over?

Getting up off the ice sounds like a good story, but sometimes you just want to lie there. You want the cold to seep through you. You want to stay away from the fight, slither away into the wintry water, and just go away. I get that.

But there's also something to be said for pushing yourself back up. There's something exhilarating about finding your legs again. There's a finality in deciding to act. There's a satisfaction in watching that bully's nose explode. Metaphorically speaking, of course.

I'm not trying to promote violence here; I'm just trying to put my finger on that thing within each one of us that pushes us to get up and fight on. Life will show you glory, and life will push you down on the ice. It's going to happen. And no one really has an answer for why. The only thing I can think of is this: It doesn't matter what life does to you. Glory or ice, it's a punch in the gut. What matters is how you respond. What matters is never giving up. What matters is realizing the fight's over only when you stop swinging.

Hope doesn't always look like sunshine and moonbeams. I've found hope to look more like bruised knuckles, calloused fingers from playing bass guitar for hours on end, raccoon eyes from driving all night to the next gig. Sure, the sunrise may remind you that another day is dawning. But before the sunrise, we must endure the night.

BOUNCING CHECKS TO DOMINO'S

I struggled with losing Pappaw for some time. Do you ever really get over such a loss? It was a bittersweet time of life, losing him, but it was also the beginning of my first professional gig as an artist. When I laid him to rest and left him there, I was filled with sadness that he wouldn't witness what I was accomplishing at this early stage in my career. Having played such a large role in developing my love for music and teaching me how to play bluegrass,

I hated the fact that he would never be able to see any of it—at least not from an earthly point of view.

With each sold-out concert, with each nomination, I felt like I was accomplishing everything I wanted—a reality I couldn't have scripted any better—while simultaneously feeling like I had lost my soul.

I left Lee University and moved to Atlanta, Georgia, for about a year and a half and then to Nashville. I lived at 701 Airways Circle, my first apartment. But to tell you the truth, for those first few years in East to West I felt like I was on the road more than in my apartment.

Neal and I took every single gig we could. We'd do churches, youth camps, Winterfest, festivals—anything and everything. Our first major tour was with Al Denson. I had to pull double duty—no, more like triple duty.

Each morning when we'd pull into the venue, I'd help wire the monitor wedges, and then I'd pull cords all over the stage for the sound crew. It wasn't exactly what I had imagined in my mind as the glitz and glamour of being on my first "real" tour.

Then I'd take a small break, do our opening slot with Neal for forty-five minutes, have about twenty minutes of downtime, change clothes, and then play bass for Al in his band for his show. It was grueling. I enjoyed playing with those great musicians, but it was a long, arduous tour, to say the least.

But even though I was singing and performing on the road in a Christian band, I was still scraping together every dollar I could make. I've got some news for all those young aspiring musicians who want to know what life's like in a band.

It's awesome.

What I'm trying to say is it's tough and not very glamorous

at all, even as it's awesome. Even though we had produced a good album with several radio hits, we still had to work our tails off to support the record. The money wasn't rolling in. In fact, just the opposite. I was living lean, and so was Neal. Reality sets in quickly when you get off tour and you need to get something to eat but you don't have much cash on hand.

I was one of those guys who'd write checks to Domino's Pizza. And then they'd bounce. That was always fun. But I had to do that in order to eat. I was living hand to mouth every day. I sat on secondhand furniture that I had recovered with blankets and quilts I bought at Walmart. What silverware and pots and pans I did have, my mom brought down from Ohio. And every so often, throughout my twenties, she'd mail a box of groceries to me. Ironically, those boxes never contained a sack of potatoes.

My reality in those early years of being an artist? We lived on the road, pulling a U-Haul, trying to scrape together every gig we could.

I know what you may be thinking. *Jay, who are you kidding? You had a record deal. What more could you want?*

Oh, I don't know, maybe some pizza and enough money to see the dentist.

Seriously, getting a record deal isn't all luxurious tour buses and catering right off the bat. A tour bus? If you're lucky, it'll happen in a few years. If you're just like everyone else, it's a van and a U-Haul. Like other artists, we were doing everything we could do, playing every place we could play, just to make it, to support our single, and get a slice of pizza here and there.

I'm not complaining. Of course, we felt blessed and loved every minute of it. We knew we were living a dream. But it was still hard work. Especially when you're relatively unknown, like we were.

EXPANDING HORIZONS

After the first couple of years playing shows and recording, we made friends with different artists. I began to get enmeshed in the Nashville scene. It goes like this: You're out touring with different artists. You see each other at the same festivals. You attend the same local shows around town. Eventually, everyone knows everyone, or you're only one degree from knowing that guy or that girl.

I loved the community I found myself in. Everyone knew everybody. Later on, I'd see how everyone played across genres too. Session guys and gals singing and playing pop, country, rock, Christian, whatever. There was a lot of cross-pollination, and I loved that. It expanded my musical horizons. I felt like I was a sponge, and I couldn't get enough of it.

And I suppose there's a nugget of advice here for young artists. If you want to get noticed, you have to get to a place where you can *get* noticed. Sounds simple, right? But you'd be surprised by how many young artists just aren't willing to make the move to a place like Nashville or New York City or Los Angeles. Video is great, but it can only communicate so much. The world may be round, but the heart and soul of the music industry is best experienced face-to-face.

As a twentysomething up-and-coming artist, I was busy taking advantage of this blessing of a new world God had placed me in. I wasn't necessarily looking for love, but love sure found me.

Chapter 8

SOME BEAUTIFUL THINGS CAN CRUSH YOU

*You have to grow up, start paying
the rent, and have your heart broken
before you understand country.*

EMMYLOU HARRIS

One of my favorite books ever is *Kicked in the Butt by Love* by Velvet Jones. It's not a real book. It was an Eddie Murphy sketch on *Saturday Night Live*, and it's one of my favorites. It *is*, however, a perfect way to describe what happened to me in the summer of 1995. Because of the nature of the business we were in, Neal and I began to run in the same circles as other artists. We all had similar interests and schedules, so it made sense that we'd end up hanging out whenever we were all off the road.

I became especially close to one artist in particular. She was an incredible singer, and her star was on the rise. Her name was Claire. After playing some tour dates together and seeing each other around town, we discovered we had a lot in common. Those commonalities grew into a deep friendship. It was one of those kinds of friendships that gives life to your days, you know what I mean? And it was totally devoid of any dating drama, which was seriously a plus for guys—well, at least for this guy.

We loved being friends, period.

When we came off tour, we'd hang out with all our friends—friends in the bands, friends in the business. As fate would have it, we ended up singing together at the same event that winter. I was flying home to Ohio to see my family for the holidays right after the show, and she was flying home to see her family in Alabama. When we both arrived at the airport, we soon discovered that the weather in Chicago had severely delayed our flights, and so the wait was on. We knew each other well, so the hanging-out part was fine and easy. And after an hour or so, we decided to go to the bar and grab a drink.

Gasp! What? Christian artists drink?

Well, this one did, and many others I knew, and after the day we'd had, we needed one. Know what I mean?

Well, one hour turned into two, two into three, and finally the call came across the PA for my flight departure to Columbus. Saying good-bye to Claire this time, though, was different. Something deeper was there. I couldn't put my finger on it, but after spending time like that together, just the two of us, I knew I wanted more of what I'd just felt. I asked her if I could call her over the break, and she said, "I'd be disappointed if you didn't."

I called her every day—for ten days straight.

I tried to concentrate on what was going on at my mom's house with my family, but my thoughts kept drifting to her. Whatever happened in that airport bar was powerful and magnetic. I couldn't wait to see her again. When I returned to Nashville, we met for lunch. I had been around her a million times before, but now my palms began to sweat, my heart pounded, and a million butterflies played dodgeball in my stomach.

I drove her home, walked her up to her door, and leaned in to gently kiss her cheek, but she turned her head and our lips met.

It was electric.

A rush of emotions poured over me; feelings that were brand-new for me invaded all my senses. I was frozen there, praying that (1) the kiss would never end and (2) that it wouldn't ruin our friendship.

It didn't.

We both realized we had developed deep feelings for each other. From then on, we spent every moment we could together, which was tough with both of us being on the road. Our relationship blossomed into something really beautiful. And I think it took us both by surprise. It was the only relationship I can remember having in which we started out as friends first. That was special. I felt like that was the right way to do it. Start as friends and then progress.

Imagine hanging out with one of your favorite people on the planet and then falling in love with them instead of the alternative, which usually entails being attracted to someone's looks first, getting physical, and then suddenly realizing you don't have that much in common.

And let's be real. It happens all the time.

And some people find out after they get married that they don't have much in common. Then Father Time sets in, and they realize that staying together takes more than good looks, good sex, and money, which is unfortunate.

For me, this relationship was a sign from God. The whole scenario seemed like it was meant to be.

We were friends, and then we fell in love.

I'm in a band; she's a singer. We sing. We can sing together. This will be great. Right? I felt like we were Ross and Rachel from *Friends*—just meant to be. Or maybe Captain and Tennille singing "Love Will Keep Us Together" for the rest of our days.

I thought we would tour together and live happily ever after. It was all lining up. I know that sounds idealistic and Pollyanna, but that's exactly how I felt. I fell hard.

To give you an idea of how close we had become, we were even in my friend's wedding together. And to this day, I can still go back and dig up the photos from the wedding and see Claire and me together in the wedding photos—that's neat.

She was my first love. And the first person you give your heart to innocently, with no walls, no barriers—well, that's always special. You breathe deeper. You want life to speed up so you can slow down with her.

Well, then you can imagine how hard it was to discover that she was seeing someone else on the side. Maybe cheating is too harsh of a word for it, and she and I may have a friendly disagreement on this point, but I believe she, at the very least, started to have feelings for someone else.

A JOKE I'LL NEVER FORGET

If you know me at all, you know I'm rarely serious. I'm always joking. I'm always sarcastic—because, well, I love having a good time. But sometimes your fun sarcasm can come back to haunt you. I've stuck my foot in my mouth more than once.

Claire and I had been in my friend's wedding, and while back home in Columbus, Ohio, she told me we needed some time apart so she could figure some things out. It was the longest drive of my life. We both cried. I had no words.

I felt lonely in a car with someone sitting right there next to me. Little was said for hours on the trek back to Nashville from Columbus. I guess I knew we were having problems, but for me that didn't mean the end. I think for her it did.

Here's how I remember it.

I was driving home from being out for weeks on tour, and I called Claire to tell her I was going to stop by to say good night before heading home.

I missed her.

I hadn't seen her in nearly a month.

"Okay, come on over," she said.

I drove over to her apartment, walked up to the front door, and knocked. She opened the door and leaned in to hug me.

"Don't touch me," I said. "I know what you've been doing." Something to that effect; you know, trying to keep it loose.

Suddenly, she burst into tears.

But I was kidding. And before I could even say anything, she broke down.

"Who said something to you?" she said through her tears.

I stood there, shocked.

I was just trying to have a little fun, and I stumbled onto a hornet's nest completely by accident.

"I wanted to talk with you face-to-face, I'm sorry you've had to find out like this," she continued.

"Well, I suppose we need to settle in because it appears there are some things we need to talk about," I said in a stunned, emotional fog. I couldn't believe it.

We sat and talked for hours.

She came clean and told me that while I had been away, she'd started hanging out with another guy. It wasn't even anything serious; they were just going to dinner and spending time together. He was close to her group of friends and worked in the music business. Like I said before, everyone in this business knows everyone. So even though that was true, it was totally shocking.

After we finished talking, I paused and then told her, "You know what's sad about this whole thing? I was just kidding when you answered the door. I had no idea what you were doing. I was just having some fun."

She bawled again.

Well, we both did.

That night it all ended. There was no more confusion in me. It was clearly over.

I never did get a reason—I never knew if I had done something wrong. After that many years with someone, I expected some closure but received none.

I'd be lying if I told you it didn't haunt me for quite some time. Having decided Claire would be the one I'd spend the rest of my days with and then to be blindsided like that while I was on the road? That was nothing short of devastating. I had hoped she would mourn me at least a little, but she moved on very quickly. All of that time together, gone in the blink of an eye.

What I thought was a life mapped out and ready to live, suddenly disappeared with one statement in the shadows of a 2:00 a.m. conversation at her apartment on my way home: "Don't touch me. I know what you've been doing." A statement intended to be a joke.

I remember standing on that stoop of the apartment in Brentwood, Tennessee, after she shut the door behind me. I've never felt so alone as I did right then. I had just lost Pappaw a year before, and I was miles away from home, and I loved her.

For months, I didn't even have the heart to throw away the tear-soaked tissues that were in my cup holder, left there by her on the drive home from Columbus.

ANOTHER SIDE OF THE STORY

So that's the way I remember it all going down. But Claire remembers it another way. After all these years, Claire and I reconnected while I was writing this book. I wanted to get her permission to share this story, and in the conversation, she told me how she remembered it. And although she does remember that late-night conversation, she debates the details. But we've agreed to disagree.

According to her, we actually broke up before that late-night conversation. In her mind, we broke up on the way back from my friend's wedding. She says that in the car ride home from Ohio, she detailed one of the reasons for the breakup. She mentioned that I seemed to be jealous of a guy, Tim, who she was spending some time with. It was innocent because they were just friends, but she felt like I acted jealous when I'd call her from the tour and she'd tell me they were spending time together. She said I was making a big deal out of it because they had dated before—even though she assured me nothing was going on.

Claire says she even remembers what book she was reading the weekend of the wedding, which I'm told by my wife is a sure sign a girl remembers something big happening in her life. Claire also reminded me of how much she cried on the drive back to Nashville. I do remember her crying. Like I said, I didn't remove the tissues from my car for weeks after that. I just couldn't bring myself to do it. They were sacred to me—and that's not sarcasm. I loved her, and the balled-up tissues served as my reminder to work on things.

I've racked my brain, but for the life of me, I can't remember that it happened that way. Consider this: I'm traveling home to see one of my life-long friends get married. It was a momentous occasion. There was a lot going on in my mind. On top of that, we drove seven hours to Ohio for the wedding.

I do recall that we talked about a lot of really deep stuff on the way home, but again, I was driving, so I was a tad distracted and I can't remember every little detail, but I do feel like I would remember if she broke up with me. Maybe she did, but to the best of my recollection, she told me we needed to take a break and figure out where we'd go from there. It's been twenty plus years since then, so admittedly I'm bound to have screwed up some of the finer details.

And maybe here is where men and women differ on how they interpret things. And trust me, I'm not trying to make this a battle of the sexes; I'm simply trying to work this out in my book for the world to see. No pressure at all.

I do believe men and women are wired differently. When I hear, "We need to take a break and figure things out," I hear, "Let's work on things together." But for her, it translated to, "I'm breaking up with you."

Guys are kind of dull animals. We need things literally spelled out for us. If you want to break up with us, just say, "I'm breaking up with you."

On a more serious note, however, I feel like the miscommunication factored into my bitterness and confusion about the situation. Why else would I drive to her apartment after tour? Because I cared about her and wanted to work on things. I was trying to figure things out.

But she'd already checked out and moved on. Chalk it up to a misunderstanding of the sexes, I suppose. Guys hear one thing, girls another. Whatever it was, it hurt.

And then, on top of it all, what was the reason we needed to figure things out? What had I done? This was the most frustrating thing of all. Remember, at the time of the "breakup" I didn't have the information I have now—about the car ride and about me acting jealous. I had nothing.

At one point, after that fateful night at her apartment when she told me she was seeing someone else, I returned to Claire's place to get some of my things I had left there. Truthfully, I also wanted to talk with her. I still wanted some kind of resolution. We at least needed to talk. It couldn't just all end in the blink of an eye. We were best friends!

Something needs to happen here, I thought.

And it really did. After that night, I was in sad shape. I lay in my bed for a week. I could barely get out of it to walk down the hall to the bathroom. That's how badly this whole thing rocked me. I was depressed—legitimately depressed.

So I drove over to her apartment.

She was home. I knew it because I could see her car. I parked and walked up to the door. And then I heard them.

Their voices came from out back. The back of the apartment had a privacy fence and gate so they were walled in back there. When no one answered the door, I walked around back. Claire's sister had come to town to visit, and they were talking.

I heard Claire say, "If Jay calls here today, don't tell him I'm going out with him tonight. I don't want to hurt him any worse."

I lost it.

I unleashed a profanity-laden tirade on both Claire and her sister. Her sister stood up and tried to calm me down, but it didn't work. Since Claire had left me hanging with no closure, overhearing her instruct her sister not to tell me where she was going if I called sent me over the edge. It wasn't closure, as in discovering what it was that made her want to move on; it was the push that sent me spiraling out of control.

I stood motionless, not really knowing what to say. Begging

God, in my mind, *If there's ever going to be divine intervention, can it be right now? Can you come down here and let her know what she was missing out on in a life with me?* Alas, he must have placed a "Gone Fishing" sign on the window of his office in heaven, because the prayer wasn't answered.

RECONNECTING

In the mid-2000s I was invited to Los Angeles to speak at a music conference to a group of young, up-and-coming music executives. They wanted someone to offer some insights and points of view from an artist's perspective. As fate would have it, Claire and her husband, Rob, were there. I didn't know it at the time, but Rob worked in artist management. They discovered I was coming and decided to attend my presentation. After I finished speaking, they approached me. It was very strange to see her again after all those years, no doubt. She introduced me to her husband and told me what kind of work he was doing, and we just chitchatted for a bit. When Rob walked away and started talking to some other folks, Claire asked, "Do you have a sec?"

"Sure," I said, quizzically.

"First," she said, "it's great to see you and I'm so proud of everything you've done with Rascal Flatts! Listen, I wanted to tell you that I know this is long overdue, but I'm sorry for the way I handled our situation at the end. This has been on my mind for years. I mean, we were such good friends to begin with, and I didn't give you much of an explanation, let alone any closure. So for what it's worth, I'm sorry."

I was taken aback and, don't laugh, a little speechless. I hadn't thought about it in many years, but she was sincere, and I appreciated her effort.

I finally said, "I appreciate you saying that. It was many years ago, and a lot of water's gone under the bridge. I'm happy that you're happy and it's really good to see you and meet Rob."

Did I get a long overdue apology? Yes.

Did it make me feel any better? Maybe on some levels.

But here's the thing—would it have mattered at the time of the actual breakup if she'd said *anything* to me to try to give some sort of explanation or closure?

Truth is, no.

I would not have been able to rationally process it in any mature way because of the simple fact that I loved her and didn't want to let her go.

CLOSURE

I'm happy to say that Claire and I remain friends to this day. Although it hurt at the time, she told me she didn't think I was ready to get married.

"Jay, I just saw how you were living—not making much money and bouncing checks at Domino's Pizza. I thought, *Good Lord, if he asks me to marry him and we're both struggling artists, who's gonna support who?* It just really scared me."

Good ole Domino's.

I really can't blame her for that. No one likes to start their future together with so much uncertainty. Claire wasn't materialistic. She wasn't wanting to marry some old, rich guy and have millions of dollars. But I think that when she saw me in the van pulling a U-Haul trailer, barely making it, she probably got scared because she knew I was going to ask her to marry me.

As I reflect on the whole thing, in a lot of ways I'm grateful for what Claire and I went through because it helped shape the person I am today. There is goodness that came out of it, but there are a lot of things I wish I wouldn't have had to live through because of it. That's the reality of the situation. And it's the same way—at least I believe it's the same way—for most people who experience deep love followed by profound heartbreak.

That's what it was for me. Probably because she was the first person I ever gave my heart to with total abandonment. I loved without thinking. And I leaped without looking. But after leaping so far with Claire, I had trouble trusting again. I had trouble loving with that same total abandonment. Is it any wonder?

I think the brunt of the pain comes from me being suckered into what I thought was the right thing. The true thing. I tried so hard to play it by the book, to do what I thought Christ expected of us. I guess it hurts that it didn't turn out the way I thought it would, even though I walked the line. Still, I'm glad we walked it. I don't blame Claire for this. She followed her heart and did what she thought was right, and in the end, God had different plans for us.

She got married to a great guy, and they have a wonderful family now. And I'm happily married to Allison, and we've got two beautiful kids, Maddie and Dylan—and they are my heart.

I carried that unresolved pain for a long time. The pain cut the deepest early on, because I never knew why the bottom dropped out so easily on a relationship that I thought was rock-solid.

From my experience, too often what hurts the most is the empty air between those we love, and the things we leave unsaid.

Relationships aren't part of life; they *are* life.

They can give life, and they can take it away.

And when you're close to someone for a long time and it ends, something inside you ends too.

Strangely, I'm grateful to Claire. She pushed me and made me resolute in the fact that the next time I fell in love with someone, they wouldn't see some hapless, struggling, check-bouncing schlub. But the chipping-away process hurts. And I know it's a cliché, but the chipping makes us stronger.

Maybe it's only cliché when you're in it and someone says that to you. The only thing you want to do during the hurt is break something. It sucks. That's all there is to it. And maybe it's the years between the hurt and the present—the right now—that make it not sound cliché. Because you lived it. You felt the pain. You endured the healing process. Sure, there are scars, but they look kind of beautiful now. If this beauty mark is a cliché, I'll take it all day long.

It's on the other side of moving on and growing up that we can see how strong we've become.

Chapter 9

MY DOWNWARD SPIRAL

"Anger turned inwards."

SIGMUND FREUD'S
DEFINITION OF *DEPRESSION*

The pain of the relationship devastated me. I spent the next year and a half doing what? I really don't know. Not much of anything, really. Waffling around socially. I was depressed.

Of course, I kept at it musically. I was still touring. Still keeping some semblance of a social life. Neal and I recorded our second studio album and released more singles. We enjoyed some further radio success in the Christian music industry. By all accounts, East to West was thriving. But on the inside, I was dying. Or maybe not dying—maybe it was just a dead feeling.

I'd felt lost when I lost Pappaw. And yet music sustained me. I knew by doing music I was doing something Pappaw would've loved to see me do. There was consolation in that. But I wasn't the same. Not really.

I spun out. I made poor choices. I let go of the reins of my faith a bit. I was "in that temper" the poet John Keats describes as "if I were under Water, I would scarcely kick to come to the top."[1] In such a state a person acts; they don't think. They tend to live out the definition of *impetuous*.

CHANGED FOREVER

It was a normal day, and I needed to run to the mall to buy some T-shirts. When I got there, I walked into the Gap. I don't remember the store being busy at all. While I was picking out the shirts, I met a girl who was working there.

She was a very pretty blonde girl, bouncing around—someone who had an immediately engaging personality. Her name was Maggie. We flirted a bit, and the next thing I knew, we were dating. I had no background with her—it was totally a chance meeting. And I didn't really want to be in a relationship at the time. But it felt good to be with someone. We really just started to casually hang out; then it turned into something more consistent, and we began to date.

We dated for about a month, and during that time, we started to talk about having sex. Now, I wasn't a virgin at that point in my life. While I take full responsibility for my own actions, I struggled with this decision because a big part of me wanted to wait until I got married to have sex again. So this didn't feel right to me. Nevertheless, I caved, and one night we made love.

When we'd finished, I realized something terrible.

My condom had broken.

SO MUCH IN THE BALANCE

I sat on the bed holding my head in my hands, moaning. But I couldn't help it. We'd had sex one time, but I knew it. I knew she was pregnant. It was just a feeling, but it was that pit-of-your-stomach feeling when you know something big just occurred.

The moment to her was normal, familiar.

"I've had condoms break before. I'm on birth control. Just calm down."

"I'm sorry, I'm sorry, I didn't . . ." I couldn't even complete the sentence.

She didn't speak to me much after that. I didn't blame her for that.

But making a mistake like that was hard for me. I felt like I was trying to be good. I was in a ministry, and I took that seriously. I'd made the commitment to God and myself that I was going to wait until I got married and do it right, because I wanted to honor what God had given me in East to West and the music world in general. I knew this kind of behavior wouldn't fly—especially if my premonition came true.

The entire moment felt overwhelming. So much hung in the balance of the outcome of my actions that night. I was scared.

CONGRATULATIONS, YOU'RE A DAD

The feeling I got that night after my condom broke was the truth washing in on me like an unwelcome wave right after you've picked yourself up from the ocean floor.

Bam. Another hit.

Down to the floor you go, gasping for breath.

I don't know how I knew it that night, but I did. I just knew it—in my heart, in my soul. I can't explain to you how, but I knew she was pregnant. And that night on my bed, when I sat there with my head in my hands, freaking Maggie out, I had never felt that low—ever—in my entire life.

She left that night because I was acting so strangely. And after she left, I didn't sleep. I stayed up worrying—scenarios playing over and over in my head.

To say that the situation threw me for a loop would be to grossly understate the situation. As you can imagine, this new pregnancy with a girl I wasn't really serious about—while playing in a Christian band, playing in "Christian venues," singing about "Christian" themes—created quite the tension. I thought my world was going to end. Everything I'd worked so hard to achieve was threatened.

The next nine months were filled with panic and fear. I didn't know how things were going to play out with Neal. *How am I going to explain this to him? How will he respond? What will happen to the group?*

And what about my record label? What will they do when they find out?

It was unreal for me to think about it. It was one night. One time. One in a million chance of a plan gone awry.

Chapter 10

LOSING MY WAY

You build on failure. You use it as a stepping-stone. Close the door on the past. You don't try to forget the mistakes, but you don't dwell on it. You don't let it have any of your energy, or any of your time, or any of your space.

JOHNNY CASH

When I got the news from Maggie that she was pregnant, we were both in shock. She had completely remembered my reaction the night we'd had sex and how freaked out I was. I think she was surprised that I had predicted it so perfectly. But again, I just knew that something had happened.

We discussed many options, including getting married and raising the child ourselves, but we quickly determined we'd be making that decision for the wrong reason. Abortion was never an option, so we began to discuss adoption.

It became evident that Maggie wanted nothing to do with me. There was no interest in the two of us somehow working things out so we might raise our child together.

I didn't tell people at first, except, of course, my mom. I told Mom early on, but I sat on it for a good bit before I told anyone outside of my family, because I knew it had to be handled delicately.

When I told Mom the news, her response ran true to form.

"I know it seems dark and hopeless," she said, "and you feel like you really screwed up, but you will get through this, Bubby. This will not define who you are moving forward. And we will figure this out together. But you cannot sit around and beat yourself up and allow yourself to let this defeat you."

She was quick to look past my indiscretion and instead offer to contribute to the solution—and at one point, she did propose that she adopt the baby. That's how much my mom cared, that's how strongly she loved.

As an aside, when I reflect on the faith of my mother, I'm humbled by her show of strength—not just for me during that specific time, but over the course of her life. She had to be so strong, so often and for so many other people, that it would take its toll on anybody. And I think she was able to be strong like that because of her beautiful outlook on life. Her faith produced that vision for her, and it's that kind of faith that I desire for my own life. It's that kind of faith that I believe forms the foundation for an unshakable hope in me even to this day.

I knew I had screwed up. And it was all I could do to look past the screw-up. But my mom helped me navigate those feelings of inadequacy, despair, and failure. But even though Mom was there to offer words of encouragement, it was still a dark path to walk. And it would get darker the further I walked it.

I told Neal next. Neal was an awesome friend—and I found out in that moment just how awesome a friend he really was. He cared for me first, before any of the music stuff.

When I told him, he simply said, "I'll love you no matter what. I don't care what happens to the band as long as you're going to be okay." And he proved it through his actions. He loved me in spite of me, which spoke volumes to me, because that one act on my part basically tore apart everything he and I had worked for. It was no small thing, and I felt every ounce of the weight of it.

A few months later, there were some show dates for East to West that we needed to honor. Neal played them with another bass player. I went to watch them rehearse—and that was hard on me, but it was the right thing to do. After Neal played those shows, he returned to Nashville and we met for lunch. He wanted to meet because he had something he wanted to talk about. I couldn't imagine what it might be.

"Jay, there's something I've dealt with my entire life," he said. "This is a very difficult decision for me, but I've lived in bondage most of my life with regard to this thing."

Neal went on to tell me that the decision he was making was to finally come out. He was gay.

Now you have to understand, this was the 1990s. The reception to such news was not like it is today. Gay marriage was not yet legal nationally, and being gay was still very much taboo in the Christian world. It took an immense amount of courage for Neal to share this with me. I guess he felt a bit liberated now that I had messed things up in my own life. And I'm glad he did.

That was the end of East to West for all intents and purposes. I believe the record label was willing to go with Neal as a solo artist, but it never came to fruition. I felt responsible for our demise and wanted Neal to do what was best for him. I would have never begrudged him becoming a solo artist. The actual end of our band came as a result of an anonymous phone call to our record label—someone saying something about Jay DeMarcus getting some girl pregnant, I believe. Nothing like getting sucker-punched by someone hiding behind anonymity.

You work your whole life toward one goal. You practice countless hours, make huge sacrifices, move away from your family, and it can vanish with one phone call—that's a gut punch.

In an instant, everyone in the Christian music scene who'd had anything to do with me virtually vanished. My record label dropped me; my booking agent released me. And management? You guessed it. That's not to say I didn't have some true friends during that time, but for the most part, everyone scattered.

I understand, I guess, but it does seem that many Christians all too often kill their wounded instead of taking time to be there to help pick someone up, get them back on their feet, dust them off, encourage them, and tell them that no matter how badly they've failed, they're still loved, still forgiven.

It doesn't take much to give someone hope.

It wasn't easy to recover from that. Up to that point, I'd worked my whole life to live the dream I was living. I worked hard, for sure. But I trusted people. And I got burned. How do you put into words the kind of betrayal you feel when everyone you thought meant something to you in your life suddenly leaves—and there you stand, with nothing?

But all this fallout? That's only what happened to me. And there was more than just me in this equation. There was the anticipation of learning who this little person was going to be. There was no special baby shower day, no little celebration or "reveal" of our baby's gender because, quite frankly, Maggie and I both felt stuck in a situation that neither of us wanted to be in. I learned the baby's gender one day when Maggie called.

"It's going to be a girl," she said.

A baby girl. My baby girl.

My heart stopped. And even though the sadness of the situation lodged in my twenty-four-year-old mind, there's no denying the infusion of love a person feels—the immediate connection—when they hear the identity of their child.

Sure, the "deed" of that night marred my career, but only because of the industry I was part of. The "deed" aside, what about this new baby girl? What about my daughter? What about my relationship with her mom?

Sadly, I never had a chance to meet my daughter. From the very beginning, I wanted to be in her life. But her mother, Maggie, didn't want either one of us in her life. That was a hard pill to swallow. I understand that sometimes life sends us reeling because of unexpected situations. But my heart in that moment, though scared, still desired to be in this beautiful child's life.

The real heartbreak is that I never got a chance to be in her life or even meet her. There isn't a day that goes by that I don't wonder about her—what she's doing, what her favorite ice cream is, what her favorite movie is, where she goes to school. Does she know who I am? Does she like music?

My heart finds satisfaction in knowing that she ended up with a wonderful family, but I've had to live with this my entire life. The adoptive family was supposed to give her a letter when she turned fourteen explaining that I loved her, did not abandon her, and have tried several ways to make it possible to be in her life. Maggie and I were young, and we just couldn't agree on terms, so she ultimately decided to give her up for adoption, and in the state of Tennessee, the mother has all the power. I don't blame Maggie, and I don't have any hard feelings toward her. I just wish we could've figured out a way to stay involved in each other's lives.

DEALING WITH BETRAYAL

I don't think I believed that the fallout was going to be as great as it was. Of course, I knew I was facing some life-altering circumstances. I mean, I was twenty-four and was expecting my first child with a girl I wasn't married to.

During those nine months, I didn't sleep much, and I battled depression. I knew my indiscretion had affected not only my life and career, both present and future, but other people's lives and livelihoods as well. By making that one decision to sleep with Maggie, I began a chain of events that touched the lives of many people. That felt like a tremendous weight.

I spent a lot of time by myself, trying to figure out what the next chapter of my life would look like, because I knew my Christian career was most likely over. But where do you go in life when everyone leaves you? What do you do in life when the one thing you desire goes away?

It sent me to a dark place. I wasn't ready for this type of betrayal. I wasn't ready to be that alone.

WHERE IS GOD WHEN THINGS FALL APART?

I've often wondered why God allowed those things to happen. It was a confusing time for me because I felt like I had tried to do the right thing so many times. I believed God would honor that, instead of letting me slip as far as I was about to slip. To this day, I don't think I'll ever understand why God allowed me to go so far in the other direction.

In those months and years following the pregnancy, I remember praying, "God, I spent so many years trying to serve you and do the right things. I had sex one time. Once! You couldn't cover my back just a little bit? And now I've plunged so deep into a dark depression that I'm medicating by drinking more than I ever drank, taking pain pills, going out to bars. This isn't what you wanted for me. And I've been a pretty good servant up to this point. Cut me a little bit of slack here."

I remember feeling that way. It's painful to write words like these out on the page and direct them at God, but that's how I felt. I'm just being honest.

Of course, looking back now, all those things transpired and led up to this point right now—I get it. And I understand it to some degree. But I really don't understand why it had to take all of that to get here.

It wasn't like I was out living a lie or living a double life. It wasn't like I was out betraying God all over the place. And then to have that happen with Maggie, and the pregnancy and then me not being in my own daughter's life? Why did I have to endure all this pain to get to this place?

And yes, I'm in a good place now—a great place. But who can give a good reason for why God allows pain like that in our worlds?

And not just my pain, but other people were affected by my situation. What about their pain and loss?

I don't know. It's hard for me to process. You and I are forged by the fires we have to go through. And maybe I wouldn't be the person I am today in some regard had I not endured that pain. But no matter how good I feel now, it still doesn't take away from how lonely and dismal it felt at the time. And I think that's okay—to remember the pain, to let it return, if for only a few moments, and let the wisdom gained from those trials seep into my brain and my soul.

There's a quote I remember from C. S. Lewis—you know, the guy who wrote *The Lion, the Witch, and the Wardrobe*. (What can I say? I'm a dad now—I read those kinds of books and watch those kinds of movies now.) He wrote, "God whispers to us in our pleasures, speaks in our conscience, but shouts in our pains: it is His megaphone to rouse a deaf world."[1]

Well, let me tell you something, God got my attention. I was all ears. Maybe not at the time, but eventually I did listen to his shouts. I did hear him yelling at me through the megaphone. But even when God shouts to us through our pain, it's easy to hear those shouts and walk the other way. I still made that choice. Because at the end of the day, he gives me the choice. How am I going to respond? What decision will I make when I encounter pain in this world?

When my world started to tear apart at the seams, I didn't try to find a tailor. I helped the tear get worse by making more bad decisions. I'll never know why I wonder why things get worse when I'm the one helping to tear apart the seams of my life. I suppose there's something in all of us that's stubborn—at least there is in me. Decisions, pain, stubbornness—they all contribute to the "forging fires." But when you're in your mid-twenties, you don't have the luxury of hindsight. And all those fancy reasons why God allows pain in our lives don't always make sense or even occur to us. Sometimes all you have in the moment is the pain of betrayal. And that can be potent.

I felt abandoned by pretty much everyone except Neal and my mom. My record label, my manager, my agent—sure, they all walked away from me and Neal, and the band was no more. But I also felt abandoned a little bit by God. Not to the point of blaming him for what happened to me—I've never blamed him for anything, because all of us choose our own path. And we have to stand up and be accountable for our choices—because they're ours to make. But I'd tell him, "Hey, God, this is the time when I need you more than I've ever needed you before. Can you just help me out a little bit here? Throw me a lifeline or something? Let me use my one phone call?"

Sometimes when I pray such seeking prayers, I attach to the prayer a little Mater accent—you know, from the movie *Cars*. It makes me feel better when I hear Mater pray sometimes. And yes, I'm aware that I've now used two references to movies made primarily for children.

"Hey, Hoss, anyone pickin' up there on the throne? Sure could use ya. I've been preaching aboutcha now for about ten years since I got outta skewl, tellin' everyone they could rely on ya. I need a little help here . . . I'm using my AT&T calling card here."

Kidding aside, I was disgruntled and bitter after everything that went down. And it all did go down. And I might have had a few words with God. But I think that's okay to do. In our faith, we need to be real—at least I do. I used to wonder if it was okay to question God, to get upset with him, to be real with him. Then I came across this paragraph from Philip Yancey, the author of *Disappointment with God*:

> One bold message in the Book of Job is that you can say anything to God. Throw at him your grief, your anger, your doubt, your bitterness, your betrayal, your disappointment—he can absorb them all. As often as not, spiritual giants of the Bible are shown *contending* with God. They prefer to go away limping, like Jacob, rather than to shut God out . . . God can deal with every human response save one . . .: an attempt to ignore him or treat him as though he does not exist. That response never once occurred to Job.[2]

How cool is it that God intends for us to contend with him? That's comforting for me to think about. And I wish I would have known that back in my dark times. I wonder how helpful that would be to a person in a place like I was—in a dark place, a place of despair. It's like talking to a good friend. Isn't it great to meet up or call one of your best friends, someone you know you can vent with, and just go off. And you can go off because you possess supreme confidence in their willingness and ability to hear you out, to let you go off and love you anyway. Well, that's what I think Yancey is saying here. God was that friend to Job. And he's that friend to me and to you.

It was at that time when a familiar face, a soon-to-be best friend, resurfaced in my life. I met Michael English again.

If you remember, I'd met Michael a few years earlier when I volunteered to drive him to the airport after he had performed at Lee University. He was so kind and encouraging to me about my music and my dreams for a music career. When I met him this time, however, I was on the other side of the music industry curtain.

When Michael hit the contemporary Christian music scene, he became a sensation. With an incredible voice and a commanding presence, Michael was powerful to watch and listen to. He grew up singing gospel music, and in the mid-1980s, he became the lead singer for the Gaither Vocal Band. In 1991, after Bill Gaither encouraged Michael to go solo, Michael signed his first solo deal. His first album, which was self-titled, won two Dove Awards—that's the Christian version of a Grammy Award. He won all kinds of awards over the next several years.

In 1994, right after the Dove Awards, the Christian music world would receive some disturbing news. Michael, who was married with a young daughter, had been having an affair—and it was with another very popular Christian singer. But it wasn't just an affair. Marabeth Jordan, the Christian singer with whom he'd had an affair, was pregnant.

As you can imagine, Michael's career in the Christian music industry came to a screeching halt. He was asked by his label to issue an apology, and he voluntarily gave his Dove Awards back. He was dropped by his label. And that was that. Or was it?

He spent some time with friends, and after a few years, he re-emerged. But this time, it was in the pop world with Curb Records. It was during his time with Curb Records that I met Michael.

I was an insider now, and he had just come out of his own crisis.

FINDING A FRIEND

My good friend Mark Lowry stayed in touch with me. Neal and I had toured with him as his opening act on his *Remotely Controlled* tour. We were close, and he knew I was hurting, so he checked up on me from time to time. One day, he asked me to go with him to see Michael in concert. I hadn't seen Michael in a while, and I decided to go.

I was blown away. What an amazing singer! I remember being at that concert, escaping. How wonderful it was to be reminded of the love of God and to just take a break from all the mess I was in the middle of.

After the show, Mark and I went backstage and said hello to Michael. We exchanged phone numbers and made plans to grab a meal sometime. A few weeks later, we did just that. It became obvious from the beginning that we had much in common. He knew exactly what I was going through, and even though my ordeal hadn't been as public as his, I could definitely relate to what he'd been through. We became inseparable. I even got an apartment across the street from his.

It wasn't long until he offered me a job to come on the road with him, play bass, and road-manage. Remember when I told him at Lee that I'd like to play for him after I got out of school? Just another one of those moments when life's little loose ends seemed to come full circle and tie themselves up.

But it wasn't without more drama, without another pothole.

I couldn't believe it. All of my gear was gone. My bass, my keyboard, my pedals—all of it gone. They took everything. Broke into my apartment and cleaned me out. The break-in was another wave that washed over me. I was broken, and now I had no gear. What the hell? I had just landed this gig with Michael English. Now this? *How was I supposed to do anything?* I thought.

I called Mom to tell her I was coming home. I'd had enough. Too many bumps in the road. Time to get out of town, right?

"You're not coming home," she said. "God has you right where you are for a purpose. You have to somehow dig deep and find some strength and keep going."

Mom was big on hope. And big on action. After my pep talk, she maxed out her credit card and bought me a bass so I could go make a living with Michael.

Good friends and good parents don't come around often. But we need them in our lives. We need that voice of truth, that one person who's not afraid to tell us what we need to hear, even when we're ready to pack it in. I'm fortunate in that I now have several friends who I have no doubt would tell me to get my head screwed on right and get after it, to stop feeling sorry for myself and keep going. And my mom is definitely still one of those voices. As much as I'm sure she wanted me to come home so she could see me, she wasn't going to give me permission to get out of an uncomfortable spot and lick my wounds. And I needed those good and hard words at that moment.

I bought another bass and joined Michael. We had a ball.

I was already a fan of his music, but to share the stage with him—to be there to see what an incredible gift he had—was awesome. We had a wonderful rapport on the stage together and it was just plain old fun. We played together, and we partied together.

And boy did we party.

Michael and I found a common thread and a common bond. We'd both made some bad choices that affected our careers. And we both had been hurt and betrayed by the Christian music industry.

It's easy to see the parallels between us. Michael remains one of my dearest friends to this day. He likes to tell the story of when I played bass for him and filled the water bottles onstage with straight vodka. I have to admit, that was a killer prank and one we still laugh about to this day.

But as close as we were and still are, my life during those years of touring with Michael was revealing to me.

Michael had a unique understanding of the position I was in. Michael never judged me or condemned me or anything about my past. He simply offered me friendship, which was something I desperately needed at that point in my life. Michael and I became inseparable. And though he and I have remained friends to this day, and dear friends at that, the next two years together sent us both down a dark path. Our friendship is still something that legends are made of.

BLACK DAYS

The years with Michael were tough—but also good. I was honored to work with him and stand on the stage with him. But I was also searching for what the next chapter would be in my life. As much as we enjoyed great chemistry, I felt like there was something on the horizon; I never felt permanently planted there. And yet I knew I was where I should be for that moment; I wasn't just biding my time. I loved our friendship and the music we performed together. He was a dear friend to me during a very dark time.

None of my choices were Michael's fault. I made my own decisions. I was just simply lost. I had so many questions and so many doubts. In a lot of ways, we were bad medicine for each other because we fed off each other's bitterness and discontent.

So in my disillusionment, I started to party and to drink more than I had ever done—going to clubs and being in places I had no business being in. And I guess all of that numbed the pain of the feelings—of losing everything I'd worked for. I felt a lot of guilt and pain over having dragged Neal through the whole ordeal. He was my partner in crime, and I had let him down.

Sometimes in life you feel restless, like you know you need to be where you are at that moment but knowing that something else is coming. I had no idea what was coming. I hoped for something, anything, to bring me back to a place where I could really do what God had for me. But it was hard to see through such a convoluted haze.

Those few years are a bit of a blur to me now. I did grow personally, though, because for the first time my faith was truly challenged. I asked myself hard questions: Did I really believe all those things I'd been living my life by for all these years? Or was it just the result of being dragged to church and indoctrinated from an early age? So I sort of deconstructed my beliefs, started with basic premises, and built from there.

I started with the basic belief that there is indeed a God. I never stopped believing that. Then I added the fact that all of us need help—we all need salvation. Then I started to think about that "help." That help was Jesus himself. He was brutally beaten, the flesh torn from his body, spilling his life's blood and dying on a crude, wooden cross.

That blood was shed for us. All of us. Isn't that amazing?

Even if someone chooses to never accept him, to deny he even existed at all, Jesus' blood was shed for them.

And you know what? It wasn't just shed for the times when you're going to Sunday school and you're winning "Parent of the Year" awards, when you're getting good grades in school and treating others around you with unselfish kindness—all the things "good Christian folk" are supposed to do. Jesus' blood was shed for the ugliness too.

His blood was shed for your doubt. Your anger. Your bitterness. The deepest, darkest corners of the heart that hide the vilest, most embarrassing, most humiliating thoughts and secrets you never want the world to see. It was shed for your unfaithfulness, your disbelief, your jealousies. Your feelings of never, ever living up to your potential and never being good enough.

In his eyes, you are. And that is all that matters.

I love grace.

It is the greatest, most miraculous gift ever given. You can't outrun it, outsin it, or use it all up. It has no limits to what it can cover.

I've heard some legalistic preachers talk about "backsliding all the way to hell." Well, how is that so? If grace is a gift that none of us deserve and could never do anything to earn, then how in the world can you put limitations on it?

Now, I'm not suggesting you use grace as a license to do anything you want and live life however you want, but I am saying you shouldn't live your life in the shackles of guilt and shame, walking around in constant fear that if you blow it—if you're human, if you slip up and make mistakes—God is going to send a bolt of lightning from the tip of his finger and extinguish you like the worthless piece of crap that you are.

Nonsense!

That's not why Jesus died.

God isn't just sitting on his throne with an itchy trigger finger, waiting for you to screw up. He's watching, cheering you on, pulling for you, wanting you to be the best you can be. That's your Father.

He knew we would mess up, and he loved us in spite of it.

Michael was ultimately the one to give me my first "real" gig as a record producer. After a while, he came to me and said, "I have a vision to reimagine some of the tunes I've sung all my life. Would you like to do it?"

"Are you kidding me? I'd love to do it!" I promptly replied.

So toward the end of 1996, we went in and began work recording "Gospel." It was an absolute blast, not to mention an honor. We ended up getting a Grammy nod for that record, and it has been Michael's biggest-selling record with Curb Records. Michael and I remain close, and I also produced his *Some People*

Change record in 2013. I love him dearly, and he will always be one of my favorite singers on the planet. I learned so much from him and I'm so thankful for the time I got to spend with him.

Perhaps one of the main things Michael taught me was how to extend grace to a person who was battered, bruised, and broken. And I will forever be grateful for the kindness he extended to me in giving me a place where I was wanted, where I was needed—a place that felt like home for those years.

Hope is not a sprint. It's a marathon of belief that something good will come out of this mess we call life. And in the dim corners of this mess, we can still have hope. Because hope does not require you to win at anything; it only requires that you get back out of bed, put one foot in front of the other, and tackle the day, and then another day, and then another. Pretty soon, those "dim corner" days pile up, and you realize that you're the one who, with God's help, has faced them; you're the one who, with God's help, has fought through them; you're the one who, with God's help, has gotten stronger.

And when you're strong enough? That's when you realize strength is more than muscle and bone. It's surrendering in the moment and casting all your cares upon God, because he cares for you.[3]

Chapter 11

FIDDLE AND STEEL

You'll walk the floor, the way I do
Your cheatin' heart will tell on you.
HANK WILLIAMS

Do you know what a honky-tonk is?

Me neither. And I used to sing in them all the time in my early days living in Nashville. Turns out the term "honky-tonk" is more nuanced than I thought. In one respect, it's a rough-and-tumble kind of bar that features live country music. That's the generic term. If you visit a honky-tonk bar around Nashville, you'll probably find a wide array of folks from all walks of life—white-collar, blue-collar, backward-collar, prepped-collar, you name it. It's a place where anyone can grab an ice-cold beer and cut loose while enjoying great live music.

But I've learned there's a bit more to it than that. Honky-tonks were a mainstay in the American South culture (and Southwest) and rose to prominence after World War II, and they gained in popularity in the middle of the twentieth century, around the 1950s.

You'll probably find different perspectives on the type of music that's common at honky-tonks. And it does have roots in American swing. But true honky-tonk music is highly emotive and downbeat. It wrangles with topics like heartbreak, hard living, cheating—you know, everything that country music embodies today.

And because these wonderful establishments were places of ill repute, they didn't have great gear. Much of the playing and singing were performed on old, out-of-tune pianos. So the melodies didn't matter as much as the rhythm did. You'd also hear the sounds of the steel guitar and the fiddle accompanying the old pianos. Hank Williams's "Your Cheatin' Heart" was a staple honky-tonk song. Kitty Wells is credited with bringing a woman's voice to the honky-tonk life. She sang about "divorce, drinking, and cheating" in the '50s! Ernest Tubb (the Texas Troubadour) and the aforementioned Hank Williams joined Miss Kitty as the iconic honky-tonk voices.[1]

So when I tell you that I got my start in the country scene by hanging out in bars listening to music, I was living the honky-tonk life. Living that life, hanging out and listening to some of the best live music on the planet had me channeling my dad over and over. His love was the honky-tonk life. He knew it well, and it shaped him. I think my love for honky-tonks, beer joints, dive bars—whatever name you choose to call them—rests in the raw passion I found there, and that's the same passion I watched boil over in my dad when I was growing up. I had always been curious about it and had wanted to experience it for myself, and I was about to.

After about two years of touring with Michael, doing some producing and road-managing and playing with him onstage, as well as partying hard, another opportunity found me. I had been running in a completely different circle of friends—friends who were immersed in the country music scene, friends who were really good players.

Some worked as side guys for other artists, and some were just trying to forge their own path. I'd go watch several bands, and soon I began to sit in with them. I became good friends with a guy named Preston Stanfill. He was a great drummer who happened to be in breakout country star Chely Wright's band.

One night after I had been filling in on the keyboard with a band he played drums for called "The Blue Healers," we started to tear down our gear when he said, "Hey, Chely needs a keyboard player. You want the gig?"

I was a bit confused and said, "Don't I have to come in and audition?"

To which he replied, "No, no. I've told her all about you, and I've been with her for years. She trusts me. So what do you think?"

I told him how flattered I was that he thought of me for the gig, but inside I knew I'd have to quit Michael. This gave me some anxiety. I loved playing with Michael, and I knew it would hurt him. The truth is, we weren't working all that much, and I needed to make a living. I considered all the repercussions for a moment and told Preston I was thrilled to try it.

"Let's do it," I said.

And with that I was Chely's new keyboard player.

Remember? Opportunity meets preparedness—a bit of wisdom I always try to live by.

Bottom line? It was a good gig, and steadier income. In this business, finding good-paying work that comes with longevity is like finding a gold mine. You sell everything you have, and you hop on board.

I could have stayed with Michael and continued our cycle, but I felt like I needed a change. Chely was white-hot, with her song "Single White Female" racing up the charts. Soon after I joined the band, other hits would follow. She was riding a wave of success, and I was happy to catch it and ride it with her. I was going to be on the road playing 150 dates a year or more. That sounded like the change I needed.

The hard part was having to tell Michael. When I told him I

was leaving, he wasn't happy at all. I felt bad about it, but it was the right thing for me. And eventually he came around.

But there was only one thing. I needed some keyboards, and I was broke. Do you sense a constant theme here?

Jay bouncing checks to Domino's?

Jay too broke to buy a keyboard because his got stolen?

What was I to do?

I drove down to Corner Music in Nashville and browsed the store for the gear I needed to use for Chely's tour. *How in the world would I pay for it?* I had no idea. I landed on a Korg SG ProX and a Hammond XB-2—a great setup, but not cheap. I think it all totaled around $3,000. My car wasn't even worth that much. I talked to J.D.—I believe he was the store's manager but may have been part-owner—and told him my predicament. I also told him about the robbery two years prior that cleaned me out.

"How much do you think you can scrape together for a down payment?" J.D. asked. "If you can give me some cash down on it today, I'll let you walk outta here with the gear."

So I scraped together $200 and gave it to J.D.

"Here's what I'll do for you. You come in when you get paid every week and pay me what you can until it's paid off."

I couldn't believe it. Sometimes I'd pay him $50. Other times I'd give him $100. I'd go in and pay him whatever I could spare. He knew I had no credit, but I did with him. I'd been hanging around that music store for years. He knew how hungry and desperate I was, and whether or not he knew it at the time, he was an answer to a prayer. The whole arrangement blew me away. Looking back on it now, I see that it was one of those little God moments that kept me going—a nugget of hope.

I do believe, however, that I saw the hope in the moment.

Hope is easy to recognize. It's usually wearing kindness, a jean jacket, and snakeskin boots. Well, definitely the kindness bit. Those kinds of hope nuggets kept me going at that point in my career. Now I buy most everything I need from Corner Music, because J.D. believed in me when no one else did and basically fronted me my main setup. I'll never forget that as long as I live.

KARAOKE GOODNESS

In the meantime, my cousin Gary called me to talk about his love for singing. My mom had called me one day and went on and on about how incredible Gary was and how passionate he'd become about singing. Gary and I had grown up going to church together, but we lost touch after I graduated from high school and went off to college. He was coming through town on his way to a vacation in Florida and asked if he could stop in and sing for me. It wasn't even his main reason for coming to town. He just wanted to get my impressions as he passed through town.

"Hey, Jay," he said, "I've been winnin' some karaoke contests here and there in town, and I want to sing for you so you can tell me whether or not I've got anything."

Honestly, I thought, *Oh gosh—you gotta be kidding me!*

But I responded with, "Sure, come on down!"

I mean, I was nervous. Who wants to tell a family member that they're not very good and should never try singing as a career? Which is what I ignorantly thought I'd probably have to do.

So when Gary arrived, I sat down at the piano and played something I knew he'd know. We grew up listening to a lot of the same music.

He blew me away.

My jaw was on the floor. I never expected to hear that kind of vocal prowess coming out of my cousin. He had R&B phrasing with country overtones wrapped in a gospel bow. It was the most unique blend of styles I had ever heard. What a brilliant surprise! After that, he became my personal jukebox. I wanted him to sing every song I could think of, and we played and sang for nights on end.

What's funny to me now is that not only had I not heard him sing before—and if you don't remember, we're cousins—I didn't even know he sang at all! I'd grown up with this kid and had no idea he was singing in Ohio!

Totally spectacular. I was honestly dumbfounded.

Over the next several months, Gary came to town, and we'd sing at a couple local spots. Eventually, though, I told him, "Gary, I don't know how you're gonna do it, but man, you gotta live here in Nashville." At the time Gary was still living in Columbus. But I told him he needed to move to Nashville and pursue singing so I could help him get a record deal and maybe produce for him. That was really the original plan.

About nine months later, Gary called me and said, "Okay, listen. I've got a job I've been at for ten years. I've got bills to pay, everything I've got going here in Ohio, but I'm miserable. I feel like if I don't get down there as soon as I can, I'll always regret it. God has given me this gift, and I gotta use it. So I'm gonna come to town and try it."

"All right, man," I replied. "You can live with me. You can sleep on my couch."

I had a one-bedroom apartment at the time, so the couch was the only place he could sleep. And he did it. He moved to Nashville and slept on my couch for about nine months.

I called Michael and asked him if he could give my cousin Gary a job singing background vocals, just to give him some income. At first, Michael was skeptical and probably still a tad bitter that I had left him. I understood that. But I told him, "Trust me, Michael, when you hear this guy sing, you're going to want him on stage with you." He agreed to hear him.

I was right. Michael was blown away. Y'all, Gary can flat-out sing. Not sure if you're aware. So I introduced Gary to Michael, and Michael took him out on the road with him.

FIRE YOUR BAND?

I was out on the road with Chely for two weeks when she found out who I was and what I'd done with my former band, East to West. One day on tour, she invited me to the back of the bus to talk.

"Oh my God, Jay, I had no idea you're an artist," she said. "What in the world are you doing here? Why didn't you tell me you'd had a record deal and all these hits?"

I was flattered, but I just told her, "Well, Chely, I need a job."

"I feel so fortunate to have you here. It's so incredible," she said. Then she asked me if I would consider being her bandleader. I was a bit dumbfounded. I'd only been on tour for a few weeks!

"Well, Chely, I guess I'll do it. But what about the guy who's the current music director?" She said, "Well, I've had some trouble with a few guys. I want you to hire some new ones."

"Let me get this straight," I said. "You want me to fire the guys who've been here longer than I've been here, and you want me to hire a new band?"

"Yes, that's right."

"Uh, okay, I'll do it."

Talk about awkward moments. But even more than the awkwardness of being the new guy and getting bumped up to director and firing the band was the real tension I felt at transitioning from being the artist to being behind the scenes. It was something I jumped into with Michael, and it was tough then. But honestly, those days were so dark for me and I was struggling with so much that I'm not sure it really hit me. But working for Chely now, I could feel it. And it was tough.

I don't mean this from a pride perspective. But when you're running the show, writing your own songs, and performing your songs with your own record deal, it's no small step to go from the front to directing the band and playing keys. It was a difficult transition for me. But I was grateful for the opportunity—no doubt about it—and I pressed on and did my best.

We held some auditions, and some of it was word of mouth. A hotshot guitar player named Joe Don drove in to audition for guitar player. He'd heard about the audition from our mutual friend Preston. I didn't know Joe Don from a hole in the wall, but I immediately loved his style. He drove all night from Oklahoma to Nashville to make it to the audition.

There was something about him that was just special. Something I couldn't put my finger on. He was a little bit cocky, but he played guitar and sang well; he backed up his swagger. But it wasn't just his swagger. Something stood out to me about him. Sometimes in this business you just know when something's right. And that's the way I felt when I heard Joe Don audition—I say "audition," but he actually just sat in with us and played a set.

I hired him on the spot. And it didn't take long for us to become fast friends while we toured with Chely. I still like to kid around and remind him that I was his boss for a while. We both get a kick out of that—well, maybe *he* doesn't! Do you see the puzzle pieces coming together?

My time with Chely was great. It was a much-needed breath of fresh air. She was very supportive and kind to me. We became close friends, and we remain friends to this day. I'll always be grateful to her for giving me that opportunity.

OUR OWN LITTLE HONKY-TONK

In the meantime, I was telling Joe Don about Gary when we were on tour, and vice versa. I'd get home from tour and tell Gary about Joe Don. "Man, Gary, you gotta meet this guy. He's great. He sings, and he's a killer guitar player."

At that time, we orbited one another's worlds. But we had no aspirations whatsoever to be a band. I wanted to produce Gary, write songs for him, help get him a record deal—help develop him and get him to where he needed to be for a career as a singer. Never in a million years did I dream we'd be a band.

At that point in my life, I'd already done the artist thing, and it hadn't panned out very well. And though I dealt with the transition from artist to musician and producer, I had come to terms with and set my mind on being a songwriter and a producer. I was growing more and more content to remain behind the scenes at that point in my life.

But the artist thing wasn't totally dead. There was still one thing that kept me in the artist role, and that was playing out with Gary. Gary didn't play an instrument, so when he sang out, I'd accompany him. We continued to play out together, and the more we played, the more we developed a loyal following of fans. They followed us everywhere we played. Gary's voice was unique and contagious. Once you heard it, you had to have more.

Eventually, we played at the Fiddle and Steel Guitar Bar—a place where a lot of the road musicians who played with other artists congregated when they were off the road. It was an awesome place to meet new people, to network, and to play with some of the best musicians in town. It was in an old building, probably from the late 1800s, located in Printer's Alley in downtown Nashville. The smell of cigarettes, beer, and musty stone walls was immediately palpable when you walked in through the red metal door. Everyone was there for two things—beer and music.

When we played there, we packed out the house every Monday night. One night, the owner approached us and said, "I'm thinking about buying the other half of this space, knocking the wall down, and putting a stage in. If you guys would hire a full band—not just the two of you—what do you think about committing to every Monday and Tuesday night?"

Of course we jumped at the chance. Nobody was getting steady gigs like that. The next step? Put a band together.

At that point, Joe Don was not in the mix. I used another guy I knew from the music scene. His name was Shane Sutton. Gary and I knew him from his band, the Blue Healers. Shane played guitar for us for the first few months, and he was good. In the beginning he contributed to the whole vibe we developed. We were a mixture of Top 40, country, old R&B, and rock and roll. If you requested it, we tried to do it.

We had a great time. People loved it. And so did we. And we kept packing out the place. Our success and following grew hand in hand.

The stories that mark my path inspire me when I think about them. And I believe they can also inspire someone *like* me. That's why I'm telling them. I was just a boy from Ohio with dreams and aspirations who made a lot of bad decisions, but who also followed that little voice from heaven inside him that said, "Trust me. Keep going."

When times are uncertain and you feel a little lost, it's tough to forge ahead and find your way. I know, because that was me. There were times in which the events that surrounded me seemed insurmountable. In times like that, I found hope in things like the simple kindness of J.D. and in the confidence that Chely Wright showed in me when she asked me to be her bandleader.

The J.D. event was one of many in which I thought I was stuck and there'd be no way I could move forward. Losing my band and my career and having a kid were monumental things for me. And I was only in my twenties at that point. When you're in the moment and the desperation is so thick you feel it smothering you, that's the time to pray for help and open your eyes wide. Because you never know how hope will find you. It may show up in the most unlikely places.

HONKY-TONK LIFE

You know, life is like an old honky-tonk. The old floor creaks and the bathrooms are dirty, but the beer is cold and the company is welcoming. Sometimes you and I can feel weathered and spent, like the creaking floor and the old banged-up piano. But it's out of those antique and broken-down things that we find the true beauty of living.

It's there on the sticky peanut-shell floor that we hear the honest sounds of a fiddle playing the slow bows of a sad song. And that sad song somehow brings us comfort. And it's in there, in the dim light of that shanty bar, that we hear the gritty sounds of the steel guitar as it echoes somewhere inside our hearts. It reaches deep too and reminds us that we have some fight left in us yet.

And it's standing in a room full of strangers and friends, listening to the rhythm of the music, that cheers us and carves a smile onto our face.

It's in those moments when we're caught in the heartbreaking aura of the honky-tonk that we realize we're not alone—that we're never truly alone. Isn't that something? In a place where there's so much heartache being sung about and so many sorrows being drowned in beer, there is comfort in knowing you are not on an island but are surrounded by similar souls.

There's always a song waiting to connect with our hearts. And behind every song is a heart, and behind every heart there is God. And then we realize that it's God himself who's sitting up there on the steel, keeping time with his snakeskins, and belting out that old bluesy song just for you and me.

I loved playing in those places. I finally understood what Dad must've felt when he played the bars in the late '70s. In a weird way, I was channeling him.

When the dance floor was packed and we were rocking, doing some of the same exact tunes I'd grown up listening to Dad play, I could close my eyes and almost go back in time. I could see him there in the thick smoke, that Fender Rhodes piano shaking as he pounded it, his left hand pumping out those bass lines and the sweat dripping from his forehead as he sang an Elvis tune.

People shoulder to shoulder on the dance floor, soaking in every moment, hanging on every word and every beat. In those moments, my connection to him was impenetrable, and the bond unbreakable.

Dad came in to see us a few times. He'd sit in the corner and listen intently. We were just doing covers, new and old stuff, long before Rascal Flatts existed. He'd sit back with his arms folded, and every once in a while, when we finished a song, he'd look at me, shake his head, and give me a wink and a smile. I lived for that wink and smile. It was worth more to me than all the gold in Fort Knox.

Chapter 12

THAT'S NOT GOING TO WORK FOR ME

If grass can grow through cement,
love can find you at every time in your life.

CHER

Who are you?

No, really, answer the question. I'll wait.

What did you say?

Did you answer by describing what you do? Did you answer by stating your name? Did you roll your eyes because it's a silly way to begin a chapter? Well, hang with me, because it may seem like an obvious question, maybe even a silly one. But I assure you, it's anything but.

You and I like to answer that question in all sorts of ways. We answer with our job title. We answer by giving our names. Some of us may answer with our most recent failure or our most embarrassing moment. Some of us may even share our proudest moment or moments.

"That's who I am," we say.

I think about this question a lot. Earlier I mentioned how after deciding to marry, Mom and Dad welcomed a little boy into the world who was destined to live with name confusion.

I like to have fun with the story of my name. But even though there was confusion early on, I'm proud to be known as Jay DeMarcus. A lot of times growing up, though, I wanted to be someone else, like Daniel LaRusso from *Karate Kid*; Jed Eckert, played by Patrick Swayze in *Red Dawn* (one of the best films ever made); Rocky Balboa from, you guessed it, *Rocky*; Hannibal Smith from *The A-Team* fame; or Luke Skywalker—any of these would have suited me just fine.

But locked up inside my name is my story. It's the story of a little boy who fought his way through a rich but also challenging childhood, through disappointment and through hurt, and who came out on the other side as a young man who still clung to hope, who still believed that in the end, everything was somehow going to be all right.

And sometimes "all right" may mean taking the scenic route through the Valley of Pain. But for as much pain I've had in my life, I can always look to the beautiful things—the things that make me tear up with nostalgia, the things that give me joy, the things that remind me to never give up, the things I can't live without.

The pain and the beautiful collide in this life and make life meaningful and filled with wonder.

HOW ALONE

I couldn't sleep.

I was on my back, alone in my apartment in the Bellevue neighborhood in Nashville, staring up at the ceiling.

Am I having a panic attack? I thought.

I was praying about the fact that I was so stressed-out and not really able to enjoy the Rascal Flatts ride. Since those early days at the Fiddle and Steel, we'd embarked on a meteoric rise, and boy, were we ever having a ride—I was praying that I would be found. Does that seem melodramatic? Perhaps. But it's true.

It's natural to find yourself in one of those great moments in life and look around with the desire to share it with someone. I was still bitter about the whole thing with Claire ending and was upset that I wasn't spending this time with someone. It was years ago at this point. But it's in those great moments in which you find yourself alone that the first love of your life pops up, reminding you of the loss.

"You've got to help me, Lord. I'm tired of this," I whispered as I closed my eyes, trying to keep my panicking heart quiet.

"It's been two and a half years that we've been Rascal Flatts, God. Are you going to give me someone I can share this life with?"

I mean, I had dated a few girls here and there, but nothing really took.

My prayers soon became more like outbursts.

"God, I'm in Rascal Flatts. I've got all this—this—stuff that you've given me, this crazy life. But I've got nobody to share it with." I'd just turned thirty, and the realization that I was alone was hitting me hard.

I went to sleep and woke up with all that weight and anxiety on me. And little did I know, the very next day I would meet the girl who would become the mother of my children.

FINDING MY BEAUTIFUL

We'd been out on the road for a long time. I was at my breaking point. I was exhausted. When we got back in town, we had a video shoot for our first single, "These Days." The night before the video shoot, I woke up in my little apartment with my heart pounding out of my chest. I was short of breath.

This time, I just knew something was wrong with me.

I've found from having so many of them that panic attacks can mask themselves as heart attacks. I thought for sure when I woke up in the middle of the night that I was having a heart attack.

I drove myself to the hospital and went into the emergency room at St. Thomas Hospital. Of course, when you tell them you're having chest pains, the triage team ushers you directly back and the nurses start hooking you up to machines and running tests on you.

After a long series of tests and being there for a couple of hours, the doctor came back and told me he was sure I'd had an acute panic attack. By this time, it was three or four in the morning. I was so exhausted and so spent that I called Trey Turner, who was our manager at the time.

"Trey, I don't think I can make it to the video shoot. I'm exhausted. I just had a panic attack, and I've been at the hospital most of the night."

"I understand, Jay," he said, "but a lot of things have been booked and schedules have been moved—it's no small thing to reschedule an entire video shoot."

It was tough, and it pissed me off, but I understood. I didn't feel like going. All I wanted to do was go back and rest as much as possible. I woke up early the next morning and drove to the video shoot.

They took me in and sat me in the makeup chair. Right beside me in another makeup chair sat a gorgeous blonde from Jackson, Tennessee, named Allison Alderson. To say she wasn't very warm to me is an understatement. She was very guarded and very professional. But I could tell immediately that she wasn't about to settle into any kind of small talk with a stranger whose band she was going to do a video with.

"I'll be honest, I'm not really familiar with your music."

That was one of the first things she told me.

"But I've heard your first single. 'Waiting for Midnight,' right?"

"Actually," I replied, "it's 'Praying for Daylight.' I see you're a really big fan, huh?"

That was part of our first exchange. As you can see, it was going swimmingly.

As the day dragged on, take after take, I'd find Allison on the set and sit next to her and chat her up. There was something very intriguing about her. She was easy to talk to, had a warm and inviting smile, and made a very long day easier just by being there. I wanted to get to the bottom of who she was and what she was all about. I sat beside her when we took our lunch break. I found her when the catering service walked around with little snacks between takes.

At one point I found her sitting on the back of a truck. I sat with her and talked some more. She finally opened up and started sharing tidbits of herself. After having been denied on several attempts, I was glad she did, and I was glad I put the effort in. We talked about everything from where we'd grown up to where we attended church.

Finally, when we neared the end of the day, Allison laid the news on me that she was engaged. The directors had made her take her ring off for the shoot.

That sucked the wind out of my sails.

But I was persistent.

So I came up with an evil plan to add a scene to the video so she'd have to stay longer. I approached the directors, Robert Deaton and George Flanigan, and said, "Guys, what if Allison's still here when we're singing on the tarmac and she didn't get on the plane, and we have a chain-link fence and she's standing behind it in the pouring rain watching us?" This video is now famous as the "rain video" in which we played on a tarmac while the rain poured down for our song "These Days."

Robert loved the idea. I was surprised by how much he loved it. He approached Allison and told her she would have to stay late. And she was paid for the day, not the hour—maybe she made $200? Who knows. I didn't care. They made her stay late, which meant I got to be around her for a few more hours.

We shot until about three in the morning. She took it like a champ. Maybe she was a bit annoyed at the time, but she was a good sport about staying late. I figured I wasn't going to see her again after the shoot, so I might as well go for it.

When we were getting ready to wrap up, Allison said, "Hey, I'd rather not use the Porta Potti over there. Do you mind if I hop up on your bus and use your bathroom?"

"Not at all," I said. And I helped her up on the bus. While she was in the restroom, I grabbed a piece of paper and wrote down my phone number. When she came back out of the bathroom, she said, "I had a really great time today. Thanks for letting me be a part of this."

When she finished, I handed her the piece of paper and said, "I know you're going to ask for this anyway. So here it is. Here's my number."

She looked at me and said, "Who do you think you are?"

But what did I have to lose? I was never going to see her again—what could it hurt? I mean, I was joking around with her all day anyway.

Well, she put the piece of paper down on the table, grabbed a pen, and said, "My daddy taught me not to call boys. But if you want to get in touch with me, here's my number."

Right then, I knew there had to be some kind of trouble in the relationship she was in. Why else would she give me her number? I didn't really think much of it at that point in time.

As I recall, I called her a few days later, after the first cut of the video, to tell her how great it was. I left a message. She never called me back.

But you can't hide from destiny, right?

Right.

Weeks later, I ran into Allison at a restaurant. It was so random. I'd never seen her or run into her before in my life, and there we were at this restaurant in Nashville called Green Hills Grille. I was sitting at my table, and I heard a voice.

"Jay?"

I looked across the table, and there she was, sitting at the table next to us with her mom and her grandmother. Life has a funny sense of irony. She was sitting there showing them photos from the video shoot.

"Oh my gosh! I was just sitting here telling my mom and mammaw about the video shoot and showing them pictures from it. I can't believe you're here."

So of course, after that chance meeting, I called her up and said, "Hey, it was great to run into you today. I think we should go to lunch."

I have to tell you, I was quite taken by Allison. She was the most beautiful woman I'd ever seen in my life. And when I say I was taken by her, I mean there was something I couldn't quite explain that was driving me toward her. And the fact that she blew me off made our whole relationship—if we could even call it that at that point—more intriguing to me.

And I was very persistent.

I'd call her, but she'd never call me back.

So I'd wait a few days and then call her again.

And then on another random day, I ran into her again, and

after the encounter, I said, "If this isn't a sign that we should at least go to lunch, then I don't know what is."

This time Allison called me back. "I'll go to lunch with you," she said, "but that's it. And then you have to leave me alone. I'm getting married in four months, and, well, you just have to leave me alone."

"Okay," I replied.

We met at noon at my favorite place in Nashville—a little Italian restaurant called Valentino's. We sat at the bar and chatted for a minute. Then the hostess came and took us to our table. And five and a half hours later, at 5:30 p.m., we left.

After those five and a half hours, I felt like I'd known Allison my entire life. Our conversation was easy. Nothing was forced about it. I felt a connection to her instantly—like I'd always known this person and I was just catching up with them. She was so familiar to me. I felt like we covered a lifetime of conversations in just a short amount of time. That's how familiar she felt to me.

Before we left, I picked up her left hand and held it. I pointed to her ring and said, "That's not going to work for me. We need to get rid of that."

She laughed.

"I don't know where you come up with the things you say. It's been great being with you, and I've had fun at lunch with you, but like I told you, I'm going to look at houses tonight with my fiancé."

Essentially, what she was saying was, *Please leave me alone.* I can take a hint. Somehow in the back of my mind I knew we'd eventually come back around to seeing each other again or, at the very least, just hanging out. I loved being around her. She made me feel like I could do anything when she was with me. That was a feeling I hadn't had in a very long time.

I didn't call her after that lunch. I wanted to respect her wishes. I knew she needed to sort out whatever it was that was going on between her and her fiancé. I knew in my heart of hearts that it wasn't right.

But then one day, out of the blue, Allison called me and told me she had to see me. I met her at a little place called South Street Restaurant. She had just gotten back from Jackson, Tennessee— from telling her father she couldn't get married. It was a tough decision for her. Her dad had already put down deposits. It was only a few months until the wedding.

But being the wonderful man and father he was, Robert told her he just wanted her to be happy. That was all that mattered to him. He didn't care how much money it cost him. His daughter's happiness was paramount.

Allison was telling me all this at the table in the restaurant, talking ninety miles a minute. Finally, she said to me, "I have to call the wedding off. I'm not going to get married. But I can't talk to you either, because I've got to sort out my life."

When we met that day, it had been a while since we'd talked, and I thought, *Okay, you called me all the way over here to tell me we can't talk for a while?*

"Okay," I said. "So pretty much the same thing we've been doing up to this point?"

"I need to sort out my life," she said.

How long will it take for her to sort out her life? I wondered.

A week later, she called me.

"I have to see you," she said. "Let's go to dinner."

It was unfortunate timing because I was on my way back to

Columbus when she called me. So naturally I was bummed. I had to live my life. I wasn't waiting around to see if it was okay for us to talk or see each other.

"I heard you were going to Ohio for a bit. What are you doing?"

"Uh, I'm going to spend some time with my folks."

"Don't do that. Please turn around, and let's go to dinner tonight. I want to see you."

"Look," I said, "I don't want to play this cat-and-mouse game. I understand you're going through a lot. I either want to spend time with you and be with you, or not be with you."

"I just needed a little time to catch my breath. I just needed to sort out what I'm doing with my life because this is a huge thing."

She was crying.

It was a big deal.

"I get it," I said. "But I can't see you one minute and not see you the next. It's very confusing for me."

But that night at dinner, she said, "Let's see where this goes."

We've never been apart since.

LOSING AGAIN

My appeals to heaven were answered with the resounding "here she is" on the very next day after I had prayed.

Allison is the perfect balance to me. She loves, challenges, pushes, and supports me in every way. I'm so grateful for the grace she continually shows me as I try my best to continue to be a better man. She's very patient and has to put up with a lot. The life I lead and the career I'm in aren't easy. And Allison has made many of her own personal sacrifices to be with me. Now it's hard to imagine my life before she was in it.

Who am I?

The answer to that question continues to change. I answered it one way before I met Allison. I'm answering it differently with each year we spend together. And now, with our beautiful children Madeline and Dylan, the answer continues to change.

Who am I?

Jay—not Stanley—DeMarcus.

Husband to Allison.

Father to Madeline and Dylan.

I think as we continue to morph into the person God planned for us to be, each year, each month, each day, each hour, each minute shapes us. And just as my union and life with Allison change me, challenge me, and grow me, so too do the events we experience together.

I was blessed to find another close friend when I married Allison—her father, Robert. It seems that God saw to it that I would have an older gentleman in my life—someone I looked up to, someone who influenced me in a positive way, someone I could love deeply, someone I could trust and lean on. Robert became that person for me when I married into his wonderful family.

We shared many common interests.

He was a self-made man from very humble beginnings. He identified with me, and I with him. He was a passionate football fan and a huge movie buff; we would shoot guns together, play golf, take trips—you name it. In a lot of ways, I was the son he never had, and he was most definitely a father figure to me.

I trusted him.

I sought his counsel in almost every major decision I made. He was the CEO of Kirkland's—a home décor retailer—and before that, he was an attorney. He was a smart man who had a unique ability to see situations from every angle, assessing and then formulating a game plan for how best to attack it.

I loved just sitting and listening to him, soaking up everything I could. I'm a huge history buff, and he was a Vietnam War veteran. I was mesmerized when, in those rare moments, I could get him to talk about it. He was a no-nonsense straight shooter, and boy did he love his family. Over the better part of fourteen years, our bond strengthened, and we even started doing some business together.

In the summer of 2013, his doctors decided he needed to have one of the valves in his heart replaced. The surgery was successful, and in no time, we were back at it—golfing, shooting, football games. I had my buddy back.

Then in the fall of 2016, he began complaining that he wasn't feeling well and didn't have much energy. When I'd tell him we had a tee time and he'd call me to take a pass, that showed me it was a big deal. He started to look like he didn't feel well, and friends and family urged him to go get checked out.

Thanksgiving was fast approaching, and his family was on him constantly about going to the doctor. Finally, he gave in and said he'd go the Monday of Thanksgiving week. I was on the road in Orlando, but when I arrived in Nashville the next morning, he was still in the hospital, where doctors had decided to do a battery of tests to rule out things and figure out what was ailing him.

So far so good. All the tests were coming back negative. I went to the hospital to see him. He was in good spirits; his color was back to normal; and he seemed to be feeling better. I told him to hurry his ass up, because I needed to get him back out on the golf course. He laughed as always and asked me what I was going to do.

"I think I'm going to see a matinee. I wanna see that movie, *Arrival*."

He said, "Well, you son of a gun, that's just like you to go see it without me while I'm stuck in here."

That was him.

So I left.

He was at Vanderbilt University Hospital—which meant he was in extremely good hands. I kissed Ali on the cheek and hugged everyone good-bye. I made it to the movie, and about thirty minutes before it was over, my phone started blowing up. I texted Ali that I was in a movie, and her reply chilled me to the bone. **Call me back. My daddy's not going to make it.**

Is this some sort of sick joke? What? I had just been there.

It was not a joke.

I rushed back to the hospital and ran down the hall, terrified by all the possibilities that flashed into my brain with each step. When I got to the waiting area near the operating rooms, the doctors were standing out in the hallway. One of them was crying and shaking his head.

My heart plunged into my gut and then clawed up into my throat. I feared the worst.

"What the hell happened, guys?" I said.

The doctor rubbed his eyes and looked at me with a vacant stare, like someone just took the life out of him, and said, "We don't know."

The chief of staff at the hospital was there as well. When he had received word that the team was having a hard time getting Robert to come around, he rushed over to the hospital. Now understand, the entire surgery center at the Vanderbilt Children's Hospital is named the Rascal Flatts Surgery Center. You could say we're fairly large contributors to the hospital at Vanderbilt University. When the chief of staff got that emergency phone call, saying, "Hey, we've got a situation," he came over to help. He put on his scrubs and scrubbed in. Now in the aftermath of what had happened, he stood in the hallway, visibly shaken and dripping with sweat.

It was supposed to have been a routine procedure. The doctors decided to run one last test to see if the new plastic valve they'd replaced in 2013 was working properly. To do this, they needed to do a heart catheterization. During the procedure, Robert coded on the table. The team worked for forty-five minutes to bring him back, to no avail.

An autopsy showed that Robert had endocarditis, which meant he had a small bacterial infection on the new valve. What made the whole thing even harder to deal with was that if they had caught it just three weeks earlier, he'd still be here. We'd be going golfing tomorrow. A simple antibiotic would've taken care of it. Done.

But that wasn't how it played out. It turned out that a small bacterial infection took him home to heaven.

I was devastated. Another bigger-than-life figure taken in the blink of an eye.

My friend, my confidant, my golfing partner, my buddy was gone. Just like that. There are still days I walk into our closet and find Allison crying, alone, as certain memories wash over her about her daddy. And I understand it, because some of the most random things will trigger the memory of something we did together or something he said. These are the kinds of losses you never recover from. Not fully, anyway.

I loved him so much, and the pain is still fresh. I still have my moments when something reminds me of him, and I'll break down. He and my mother-in-law, Jane, are some of the most special people I've ever known. I'm so grateful for the time I had with him. I am forever changed from having known him, and I know there are pieces of him that I'll carry inside me for the rest of my life.

Some people don't have good relationships with their in-laws. I get it. But that's not me. I'm one of the fortunate ones, I guess. Allison's dad became one of my closest friends. He was formed out of the old-school mold. He worked hard. Told it like it is. And he loved hard. In a lot of ways, I guess, he reminded me of Pappaw.

And he was fun. He was the kind of guy who'd go with you to look at cars and give you his advice freely to help you out. Then when you'd pass on a car you really wanted but hesitated to pull the trigger, he'd return to the dealership and buy the car, and he'd show up the next day at your house and say, "How do you like my new ride?" I know he's like that because he did that to me! True story.

He was one of the finest men I've ever met in my life.

But you know what? Here's one of the things that gets me. This is one of those things that reminds me that there is a God, and there is a divine purpose and providence to everything we're doing. Hang with me here; this may sound a little weird, but it makes sense to me.

While I was writing this book, I woke to a typical Monday

morning. Ali and the kids had a bunch of things to do as they were getting ready for the Miss Tennessee Scholarship Pageant. The pageant has been part of Allison's life for decades. She has codirected it with her mother for many years now, and on this day, she was getting some things done for the pageant with our kids. So I had a rare day off—no tour, no recording, and the kids are running around with their mom. What to do?

I decided to drive to the theatre and see the 2:15 p.m. showing of *The Equalizer 2* with Denzel Washington. It felt good to have some free time. It felt even better to be the only person in the theatre. Another benefit of being an artist, and I'm sure it's more than just artists who get to do this, who get to see movies at really weird times and cheer, cry, and laugh their guts out in public with no one around.

I had the place to myself. It was awesome. And the movie? Fantastic! I love Denzel. And here's the kicker. I saw the first *Equalizer* with Robert.

During the second film, there's a great moment in the action and dialogue, and I chuckled and said to myself, *Oh man, that's great—I love that.* Don't laugh. You know you talk to yourself too when you're alone in the movie theatre.

I looked over beside me. To my left, an empty seat. To my right? Another empty seat. And I thought, *Man, Robert would have loved that. That was an awesome moment—he would've loved it.* And as I said it to myself, I was overcome with incredible sadness. A deep sorrow welled up in me. And I teared up, sitting in that empty theatre.

When I was sitting there, I had a half-eaten plate of nachos and a Diet Coke sitting in the seat to my right, and my man purse (don't laugh, they're handy) in the chair to my left. And the napkins I'd crumpled up were sitting beside me as well. I had taken off my hat and was rubbing my head and my eyes because I had tears in them. As I was sitting there gathering myself, I had the sense that Robert was right there with me, telling me, "Hey, man, I'm right here. Don't worry about it. I'm always going to be right here."

And then I was calm. It was so bizarre.

I can't explain that moment, but I'm sure you've experienced something similar. It was that moment when you realize that someone you miss is never coming back. And you just wish for that one moment when you could experience that special time together.

I've become more sensitive to "moments." I don't just let them slip right on by. I try to be in them. I take mental snapshots of the details so I can recall them, relive them. I think it's so important to cherish every second you get to spend on this earth with someone you love, because you never know when it's going to be the last.

I hold my kids a little tighter and turn around for one more hug from Ali before I leave the house. I call my family a little more often.

What if I hadn't turned around in that hotel room to call Pappaw that day?

I hold on to voice mails, videos, photos—you name it—preparing for the time when I need it to get me through the missing, to get me through the lonesome.

Macabre? Dark?

I don't think so.

No, this is about life itself.

I know that time is a precious commodity, and we all run out of it eventually.

Don't get the wrong picture here. I wasn't sobbing, alone in the theatre. But I had a moment.

Two days later, I found Allison in her closet, crying.

"Baby, are you okay?"

"I just miss my daddy," she said. Then she went on to tell me how she was at flag-football practice with the kids, and the same thing happened to her. She was there watching the kids, and the moment seized her. *Daddy would have loved to have been here*, she thought. We both thought the same thing.

It was bizarre to me that within the course of three days, Allison and I felt and experienced the same thing about missing her dad. I don't know how to explain it, and I'm not trying to get weird about it, but there seems to be some kind of divine connection between those we lose and the ones who are left behind. Is it maybe that that loved one is reaching out to us from heaven, reminding us that he or she is still here—keeping an eye on us or something?

Who knows? All I know is the love is still real, and it hasn't gone anywhere.

I tell you all this to say that what hurts the most is not being ready for Robert to die. I loved him dearly. But I wasn't ready. Not like that. Not out of the blue. He should be there at Dylan's football games. He should be there with me at that damn movie.

There's always room for one more "I love you." There's never space for fights that go unresolved. I think about that all the time. I never want to leave my family in discord or anger as the last thing on my lips or in my actions. I never want to be the one who leaves them in the lurch wondering if or how much I love them. I think too of my daughter whom I've never known. Did she read that letter when she was fourteen? I'll never know.

Did I just leave my wife and head out on tour with discord between us? Was the last thing on my lips anger or love?

Life is too short to keep love bottled up.

It was too early for her dad to go. He should've been beside me in that theatre. He should've been at that football game with Allison.

To lose Robert over a routine procedure when you know the problem might have been prevented, or there was a mistake, or you didn't go to the doctor when you should have—it drives me to the brink of my emotions. I want to raise my fist to heaven. I want to throw myself down at God's feet. I want to unleash profanity-laden prayers of disgust and doubt. And I want to cry out to God to hold me, to hold Allison.

It's the preventable nature of the whole thing that digs at me the most. When doing a simple thing like getting a checkup can save your life. It's tough to stomach an outcome like Robert's. It kills me.

My pappaw was another example. His heart attack was preventable. They discovered later that he overmedicated. He made a mistake, and it led to his heart attack. Who knows how long he would have lived if he hadn't made that mistake? I don't know. But I do know that seventy years old is too young to go. Both Robert and Pappaw died at seventy.

Who knows what went through Pappaw's mind when he took his pain meds? "Well, I feel good when I take one pain pill. And today I'm not feeling that great. So I'll take two or three pills, and it should make me feel that much better." He had no idea his heart couldn't take it.

And then there's my dad's mom, Gladys. She dropped dead of a heart attack when she was fifty years old! She was standing at the sink doing the dishes, and she fell over and died. That's why I have my doctor, John Peach, on speed dial. He's a very patient man—that, and I may be a bit of a hypochondriac.

Who are you?

Me?

I'm Jay DeMarcus. Not Stanley, just Jay.

And I'm a lover of my wife and kids. I'm a bass player and songwriter. I'm a producer. I love the Bengals (shut up, Steelers fans!). I have a wife who loves me, no matter what. I have children who look at me like I'm a unicorn—made for another world. And I've loved people who have died and left huge holes in my life. And you know what? I still love them—hard. I still get choked up when I'm by myself in a place or at an event I know they'd love. And I want them back. I want them to be with me to experience a good movie, a great laugh, a precious moment.

These are the people who have made me who I am.

But what I've come to realize is that the pain I experience now from losing someone I loved comes from all those beautiful moments we spent together. And in some weird way, I feel better. I'm reminded to seize every minute of every day and every experience and love my family and my friends—hard. To pull them close. And to never leave any doubt of my love for them.

Who am I? I'm Jay.

The greatest gift I can give? Love.

Because it's the love we give now that gives our loved ones hope after we're gone.

Chapter 13

BEAUTIFUL WINDS THE BROKEN ROAD

The gift must stay in motion.

LEWIS HYDE

By now you should be able to see, quite easily I hope, that I haven't always been a good steward of all the gifts that God has given me. I haven't always managed the blessings I've had in this life. I've made a ton of bad decisions. I've been reckless at times, yes, careless—and I'm ashamed of some of the things I've done. The weight of shame can be unbearable sometimes, can't it?

I've been given so much—by any standard, more than I deserved. And this is how I show my gratitude?

Acting like an imbecile?

No regard for anyone but myself?

I can't be the only one who's ever felt this way.

And I don't think I am.

If you have any kind of a conscience, then you've felt the hole in your gut, the weight on your shoulders, the constant nagging in your brain and in your soul—signaling to you that you know better.

But being a hopeful person isn't about being perfect; it's about something much more precious.

PERFECTLY IMPERFECT

I'm often asked what it means to be a Christian. I don't find the answer to be as easy as saying, "A follower of Christ." For me it's a bit more complicated. Those kinds of pat answers tend to pass right over the nuance of things. And I hate that. I like the details. I like breaking things down and getting at the heart of things.

When I say I'm a follower of Christ, what am I saying? That I'm just like him? That I've got all my stuff together? No way.

First of all, I don't believe that being a follower of Christ is about being perfect. God doesn't expect perfection from us. No one's perfect. Jesus himself said, "No one is good—except God alone."[1] So the only perfect person to walk this earth was Jesus Christ. And the last time I checked, he was the Son of God.

Newsflash: I'm not the Son of God. Neither are you.

That's why it's called being "a follower of Christ." Because we follow after him. And boy is it a journey!

We try to learn from him and from what he says in his Word, the Bible. We try to live like him—caring for those who are less fortunate, speaking with kindness to people, confronting injustice when we see it, and sacrificing everything for one another. From what I understand about the Bible, this is what it means when Peter says, "Just as he who called you is holy, so be holy in all you do."[2] We follow Christ's lead, knowing all the while that we have his grace to fall into anytime we need it—anytime we screw up.

And trust me, I reach out for that safety net of grace all too often.

So, no, we can't be perfect. But we should pursue holiness. That's the journey we're on as Christ followers.

Pursue holiness—yes! But also, you can't set yourself up for failure. You can't think that when you fail, then you're cast off by Jesus. That's not the way grace works.

Grace covers you.

It carries you.

It helps heal you when you've fallen.

Grace beautifies the broken road.

You and I—we're flawed, broken, and screwed up, but it doesn't matter. Once you accept Jesus as your Savior, you're sealed with his blood. And there's nothing on this earth that can separate you from his love.

NOTHING.

I love these two verses that remind us of this:

I'm absolutely convinced that nothing— nothing living or dead, angelic or demonic, today or tomorrow, high or low, thinkable or unthinkable—absolutely *nothing* can get between us and God's love because of the way that Jesus our Master has embraced us.

Romans 8:38–39 MSG, italics original

I think being a Christian is a constant learning process. I don't think you ever perfect it. If you're open and willing to accept yourself as you are— screw-ups and victories alike—then it's a process that never really ends. While I was writing this book, I reflected on this truth quite a bit.

The process of growing and maturing, like a tree over its lifetime and through the seasons, looks different at different stages in our lives. When I began my journey in music, I was raw and idealistic. I lived in my passion for music. And that was enough. The world of music was opening up before me, and it captivated me. I was content to immerse myself in it.

But as I grew, life unfolded like the tail feathers of a peacock. I met new people. I fell in love. I got hurt and betrayed. I lost loved ones. I realized that life wasn't all about music. Music, as it turns out, operates more like a backdrop on a stage. That backdrop remains, maybe changing color every now and again, but it's the people in front of it who move and shift and gather on the stage of life. I realized that I needed people in my life—that I needed to love and to be loved.

And throughout all the changes, I grew into a new person each and every year. In a lot of ways, I'm the same Jay who stepped onto that stage at the King's Place on that cold, wintry night. But in more ways, I'm totally different. I've taken on new roles—husband, father, friend, producer. I've matured.

This is what life looks like. It's a stage on which the characters enter and then exit stage right. The scenes change, and with every change, you become the person God made you to be. That's why you may feel differently about something in your life today than you did five or ten years ago. Your convictions have grown as you have grown. Some things may not have seemed important before, but now they may be monumentally important. That's the way things go. We grow.

All the different phases of life bring this on—kids, marriage, different career opportunities. Your core beliefs shift, change, mature.

I guess what I'm trying to say is that you need to give yourself a break. Life is long, and it's a growth process. And following Jesus is a growth process too. He's not expecting you to be perfect. He knows you're going to grow and change.

Just keep following him.

If you're a college student and life seems huge and overwhelming right now, take a step back and look at your life stage. Take a moment to enjoy the people on the stage with you. Say "thank you, God" for the opportunities and difficulties that stretch out before you. Because life goes on, and you will grow. You will move past the here and now. Look at that, we're already moving on to another paragraph. See, life moves fast!

If you're at your mid-career stage and struggling with the loss of dreams or goals, remember, this moment will pass, and you can, if you want to, still change the backdrop a bit.

If you've screwed up and made some bad decisions, take a step back. Remember, it's not too late to make a good decision. How many times have I had to tell myself that bit of advice! Well, that advice came from my mom, but I used it often. And so can you!

And listen, here's another thing that I think is great about the Christian life. Being a Christian doesn't mean you just walk around with your head in the sand when you've messed up. Jesus doesn't want to shame you. He wants to lift you up. A little band called U2 once put a beautiful psalm of King David to music. It's called "40," from Psalm 40. I love this lyric from the psalm (verse 2): "He lifted me out of the slimy pit, out of the mud and mire; he set my feet on a rock and gave me a firm place to stand." Sometimes I think we get so determined to go it alone that we forget that Jesus is standing there waiting to help us out of the pit.

And listen, it's okay to struggle. It's okay to not understand things in life. It's even okay to question God and to be disheartened with your faith. Those are natural feelings and experiences.

Why is it okay, Jay?

Thanks for asking. It's okay because doubt and struggle help us grow and make us smarter and deepen the roots of our faith. When we doubt who we are and what we believe and who we believe in, it makes us stronger. You think I had my junk together during those dark years after I lost Pappaw and got my heart broken by my first love and had a child out of wedlock?

I was a mess. And I questioned everything. But here's a good ole saying that rang true in my life then, and it's one I still cling to now: "God's not all you need until he's all you've got." Sometimes it's necessary for us to be stripped down to our very core, free of everything and anything that can separate us from him.

My buddy Neal used to say that a lot. When God's all you have to rely on, that's when the rubber meets the road and you find out what you're made of. And I've been there many times.

FAILURE IS NEVER FINAL

Years ago, when we released "God Bless the Broken Road," none of us realized how the song would affect our lives.[3] But what I can tell you is this: the song connects with so many people because we're all walking the broken road.

I remember the first time I heard that song, it really spoke to me and hit me hard. And although we didn't cut on the record that it was pitched for, it stuck with me. The beautiful lyrics about how mistakes can be made but can lead us back to where we're ultimately meant to be really struck a chord with me. That's my story.

As you can tell by reading many of these stories, I didn't always take the path of least resistance. I learned a lot of things the hard way. There are plenty of things I wish I could say "do-over!" or "mulligan!" about. But whenever I thought I'd made the biggest mistakes and thought I'd only find disaster, somehow love came up with a way to find me and meet me where I was and pull me out of the darkness, to gently nudge me back onto the broken road, to get me to where I was supposed to be. And once I was back, I discovered a place of restoration.

It's hard when you're in the middle of a crisis to believe that someday you'll look back and see that everything will work out the way it's supposed to. So I'm not preaching and would never presume to say I have all this figured out. But I do know, speaking from personal experience, that failure is never final.

It's crazy when you're in the middle of hard times to think that you'll be okay. Fear grips you. Sadness surrounds you. But those feelings can only last so long. They are temporary. Nothing stays forever; it will pass. I don't know it all, but if my personal experience has taught me anything, it's this: failure is never final.

We all have our own version of the broken road.

The potholes of mistakes.

The speed bumps of bitterness.

The roadblocks of failures.

Your road looks different from mine. But eventually, if we trust, if we keep our faith, if we keep believing, if we keep trying, if we keep pressing forward, we'll find that God is faithful, and he will meet us right where we are.

HOPE IS A GIFT WE GIVE

Whenever we sing "God Bless the Broken Road" live, I feel like it's a spiritual moment. It's unlike any feeling I've ever had. Thinking about all the people who've been touched in some deep way by one of our songs—whether it's a wedding, graduation, or funeral, or just jamming to the tunes in your car with the windows down, singing your heart out—I can see how those times stack up into a beautiful memory for each person singing the song.

And I never take that lightly.

It never gets old hearing you sing along with us.

Touching someone with the gifts God has given us is still very special, even sacred, to me. I understand that very few people get to feel what I feel every night. It's a privilege to do something you love so much, when you know there are so many people who go every day to jobs they hate. That's a reality not lost on me. It's a privilege I never take for granted.

Despite what some may think, it's not just me and the guys up there playing and singing. It's everyone—the whole stadium. It's you, singing along with us. Feels kind of like church in a way. When everyone stands and sings the old hymns together.

Those feelings I had at the King's Place during that first performance have carried over to now, and they're not really much different from that first night. And those feelings rise up and remind me of the path I took to stand right there on the stage with the guys. It's not lost on me what I'm doing up there. It's a spiritual experience, no doubt about it.

It's spiritual in that sometimes I feel like we've been put on the stage for people to hear what we're going to sing about and talk about that night. I feel like a steward up there, stewarding my gifts and abilities and opportunities to use them for God's glory. And that means not only putting on the best show we can, but also dialing in to that crowd and digging into our souls and showing them a little bit of the hope that's inside us.

I'm standing there playing my bass, playing the keys, singing with Gary and Joe Don, and doing my best to communicate the hope that I myself have sought my entire life, the hope I've found in my faith.

I would never be so bold to suggest that we get it right every time. But I do feel the weight of the responsibility of making sure we never take being onstage too lightly. Maybe there's someone there who needs to hear what we're saying, what we're singing about—someone who needs to hear a little bit of hope, a little bit of encouragement to keep going. That's the spiritual part of performing for me.

A buddy of mine told me about a book called *The Gift*. He read this quote to me, and I want to share it with you. It's the quote I used at the beginning of this chapter: "Having accepted what has been given to him . . . the artist often feels compelled, feels the *desire*, to make the work and offer it to an audience. The gift must stay in motion."[4]

Don't miss what that first phrase says. Artists must accept, they must receive, the gift. I call this part "receiving inspiration" for a song. When I accept that inspiration and allow it to set in motion the creation of a song or arrangement, it's natural for me to want to give it away. I want that new creation to go out from me to you.

There's no greater feeling than when a song connects with the listener. And that's what I experience at our concerts—thousands of people singing a song that resonates, that touches them deeply, that connects them to their friends and loved ones. The gift that I received and then gave through song then becomes your gift. And it's up to you to allow that gift to work its magic on you.

Remember, the gift must stay in motion.

Your gift needs to stay in motion too.

What do you mean, Jay? I'm not onstage every night, you may say.

You may not be. But it doesn't matter what you do. I guarantee there are people around you—in your school, at work, in your church—who need some encouragement, who need some hope. It isn't that hard. Because people everywhere are hurting; you don't have to look very hard.

We all have the same questions, the same disappointments, the same disillusionments. Wouldn't it be worth it just to touch one person's life?

What if you are the seed of hope that someone desperately needs, someone who is at the end of their rope?

Don't ever think you have nothing to offer. Shut those voices up. You may be the one working in a music store who sees a kid walk in with not a dime to his name but decides to take a chance on him, to give him hope. And because you see how hungry he is, you let him take some gear home just based on his word.

Or you may be a high school teacher who, by all rights, should fail a young man because he's flunking out of your government class. Instead, you see something more in him. You believe he's destined for other things, so you pass him just because you sense that something, someone, is nudging you to do it. (Happened to me. I'm forever indebted to Mr. Charles Zaffini!)

The point is you can make a difference right where you are. You don't need a stage.

Chapter 14

ETERNAL SADNESS OF A SATISFIED SOUL

You cannot swim for new horizons until you have courage to lose sight of the shore.

WILLIAM FAULKNER

remember it like it was yesterday.

I sat at the piano, surrounded by new faces. Faces with unknown stories —at least unknown to me. These people playing all around me were complete strangers. Danny was playing with us, and every now and then, he'd bark out something like, "Let's go, pay attention."

We played in a room that felt strange to me, but the good kind of strange. You can probably imagine a simple classroom-type setting but with instruments and a piano and some sound equipment. It wasn't church, and it wasn't my home back in Ohio.

It was an environment that spoke to me and told me it was okay to tap into my passion, to be at home in learning more about music and expressing the gifts that God gave to me. Long gone was my church sanctuary. Or at least it felt that way. In those musical moments, I experienced an epiphany. You know those times when you're doing something and you're engrossed in the moment, and the world suddenly stops spinning and you can see it for a brief moment in slow motion. It's like your whole life stretches out before you.

Right then and there, the world stopped, and I saw myself for who I truly was—a musician.

It had only been a week since I had met Danny at that youth conference. And there I sat, playing piano with strangers, grinning from ear to ear, realizing that this is what I was going to be doing, in some capacity, for the rest of my life. School was a few

weeks away from starting, and because the dorms were full, I had
to move in with Danny.

For my first six months at Lee University I lived in Danny's
spare bedroom. I remember meeting Jeff, who acted as my "chaperone" when I first arrived on campus. He was Danny's nephew
who traveled with and ran sound for the team. He showed me
around Cleveland and Lee.

It was a crazy first few weeks. Danny gave me a list of twenty-five
or thirty songs that I had to have ready for the tour the next week.
It was a tough assignment, but I relished it. Danny gave me two or
three days to "woodshed" on that song list—spend some isolated
time working hard on learning new songs in the studio close to
campus called Harmony House Studios. I came alive in the studio as
I worked on those songs. And a few days later, we started rehearsals.

I remember seeing those singers I had seen onstage at the conference arrive at the studio for rehearsal and thinking how cool it
was that I was with them now, playing with them, singing with
them, rehearsing with them. It felt surreal but also very natural.
I was not just with them; I was one of them.

My buddy Neal wasn't in the group at that point, but he would
join a year later. Javen, the guy I had spoken with first that night at
the conference, gave me a big hug when he saw me and said how
funny it was that God worked the way he did.

It's so true. He does work mysteriously.

God had moved, and in less than two weeks, I was there.

To this day, Javen Campbell—my first college friend—remains
a true friend. We never skip a beat. We can get busy and not talk
for a year or two, and when one of us calls the other out of the
blue, we always pick right up where we left off. To me, that's a sign
of true friendship.

Over the years, I've often asked myself, *What caused Javen to talk to me at that conference at Winterfest?* I puzzle over that question.

While I was writing this book, I called Javen and asked about it. He said, "Man, it seems like a lifetime ago. I was on the stage tearing down our gear, and there you were, standing there asking all kinds of questions. I think the main thing that struck me about our conversation that night was your interest in what we were doing. You were so interested in the details of our set, the gear, all of it. I could sense a serious love and desire for music in you."

And here's one thing I forgot.

He asked me, "Do you play?"

"Yes," I said. "I play piano."

But then he followed it up with, "Do you play good?"

And how did I respond?

"Yeah, yeah, I think I can play pretty good."

He reminded me about that response. And it's striking to me that I had that much confidence. That confidence is probably what got me the job and propelled me on this journey ever since. But I won't take credit for it all myself, because I know better. I know there was something else at work.

"When I think about that moment," Javen said, "I think how it was a total God moment, without a doubt."

DON'T MISS THE GOD MOMENTS

A God moment. What is that?

Have you ever experienced a God moment? I think from here on out, I'm going to call all the times in my life in which hope floats to the surface and reminds me to keep plugging away and to not give up "God moments."

A God moment—simple and subtle nuances in which you see the hand of God move, and you know it's the hand of God because who else could make that happen in that kind of way in that kind of timing?

Javen said he remembers how different it was to meet someone who played piano by ear. "We talked about how you could play by ear," he said. "That was a rare commodity back then. Most keyboard players we ran into played strictly by reading music. I remember thinking that I had found our next keyboard player after our brief conversation."

Back in Columbus, the thought of doing something professionally with music always seemed so far-off. I desired it, but it felt like an unreachable dream. Don't get me wrong. I still wanted it and pursued it. But aside from the night at the King's Place, the goal felt so hard to achieve. Yet at Lee, a switch inside me turned on that day while we rehearsed.

I have to do this for the rest of my life, I said to myself as I sat there playing with the group in the studio. It was a defining moment. Everything in my life that I had lived so far was the "before," and now I'd be stepping into the "after," where I knew with unshakable clarity what I wanted to do with my life.

But on the other side of that feeling was the reality that I was alone and in a new place—now it was up to me. At that point in my very young life, I'd already made the hardest decision I ever had to make. Moving away from home, away from everything I knew and loved. Away from my mom, my dad, and my sister.

What had I done? Was it going to be worth it? How would it pan out?

Impossible questions to answer—impossible, that is, without some kind of movement on my part. Questions that required me to get in my car and drive to a college I'd had no plans to attend. Questions that kept me moving down the line of life. Questions that move me to this day to keep going, to try it out, to see what happens.

Despite these questions, it's the God moments that keep me moving forward.

I think God moments drop in our laps more often than we realize. The problem with God moments, the way I see it, is that they generally come with a caveat. And that caveat is the requirement to do what the crazy disciple Peter did on that stormy night out on the sea.

His God moment?

It was seeing Jesus, God's Son, walk on the water.[1] Talk about a God moment. Peter had two choices: (1) sit there getting soaked in the rain and marvel at the dude walking on the water, or (2) join him. If you don't know this story, I recommend it. It will either inspire you or really freak you out.

Peter calls out into the storm and says, "Jesus, if it's you, tell me to come join you!" (my paraphrase).

So Jesus called him out onto the stormy waters. And for a brief few moments, Peter walked on the water. And then he took his eyes off Jesus, and fear crept in. And he sank.

I wonder what that felt like. As far as I can tell, only two people have ever walked on the water with any kind of success: Jesus and Peter. People like to give Peter a hard time for sinking, but he had the guts to at least get out there and try it. He got out of the boat. Jesus didn't really say much about the feeling. Probably felt normal for him to be out there. He created water, for crying out loud. But for Peter, I wonder if it felt like standing in front of an anxious crowd as a nobody keyboard player?

Peter's God moment was epic. And it just showed up out of nowhere—literally. And Peter seized that moment, stepped out of the boat, and walked on the water.

He sank, but he still seized it. And Jesus was still there to pull him up.

HOPE IS NOT A STRATEGY

Randy Goodman signed Rascal Flatts to our first record deal. He was the president of Lyric Records. I remember early on sitting in a meeting with Randy and the guys and some of his staff. One of the marketing staffers made a comment about our new single, saying they hoped it would do well.

"Hope is not a strategy," said Randy.

I've spent a lot of time talking about what hope is in this book. I've shown you hints of hope in my life. I've tried to paint a picture of what hope looks like. But there's another side of hope I haven't talked about.

What hope is not.

So let me be clear about what I'm not saying about hope.

Hope is not a strategy. You can't just hope something into existence. It requires hard work. It requires you and me to do something. Maybe it means practicing a little longer on the piano or staying after practice and working with your quarterback or field hockey coach or taking that extra course or getting that graduate degree. Maybe it means putting it all on the line day after day, working your fingers to the bone to get that promotion you've been eyeing for years.

Hope requires deliberate action. It requires us to be proactive in the pursuit of our dreams. For me, it was about practicing on the piano when everyone else was outside developing their athletic skills, playing football, or spending their summer days at the pool. It was realizing that if I wanted to be able to do something—anything—with music, then I needed to be good at what I loved.

And the only way to get good is to practice. Practicing consumed me. I spent all my time locked in my bedroom learning all my favorite riffs by my favorite bands, rewinding and replaying each cassette tape (yes, we actually listened to music on something other than a phone or an MP3 player!), trying to figure out every nuance of how tracks were put together. I'm sure some people even called me a nerd or music geek at times because I was swallowed up by it. I wanted to be the best I could be. And once I started to understand the world of music and its possibilities, it was exhilarating.

Once my mind grasped the musical concepts I practiced, I started to see all the possibilities with chord structures and melodies. I could create at will because I was forced to play by ear—it was liberating. I could experiment and try different things because I wasn't tied to a piece of music. It was fun to play whatever popped into my mind.

I'll admit there were times I wanted to be outside working to become a better athlete. God knows I needed it on the basketball court—as evidenced by the time I stole the ball and dribbled the wrong way during a basketball game and scored for the other team. I thought the team and the fans in the stands were shouting, "Go! Go!" But they were screaming, "No! No!" You can imagine how popular my fifteen-year-old self was after that fiasco.

Now I *did* have very good hands. My dad worked diligently

to prepare me to be the best football player I could be. I wanted to be Cris Collinsworth. I have very soft hands and could catch a football as long as it was thrown anywhere in my vicinity. But alas, my football dreams would never come to fruition. I played a little bit of intramural football in high school and college on different teams, but I went to a private school that wasn't big enough to have a football team. I don't know if I or my dad was more disappointed that I didn't go to a bigger school. He ran drills with me day in and day out. We had our own playbook, and he made me run routes over and over again.

That's one of my only regrets, really. I love the sport so much that I would've liked to have seen what I could have done on the field if the circumstances had been different. I blew up my knee too, which didn't help my cause. See? I couldn't hope my football career into existence.

Sometimes I hear, "Well, God just hasn't opened a door for me yet." I believe God does open doors and windows and even the hood of my truck. But I'm not so sure God opens doors for people who are just sitting around waiting for something to be handed to them.

My friend Tim told me that God doesn't move parked cars. I agree. If my car would have stayed in Park and I hadn't moved forward that night when I met Danny at the conference, I would have never ended up where I am today.

What I've learned is that you have to be willing to put in the work in order to find yourself face-to-face with an opportunity you're ready for.

"If you're lazy, don't come crying to me about things and how they haven't worked out." That's what Pappaw used to say. I think Pappaw's intolerance for laziness rubbed off on me. I detest laziness. I know that may sound harsh, but it's true. And I detest it in myself when I see it or sense it rising up in me.

In my mind, I was willing to do whatever it took to accomplish my dreams of being a musician. I didn't know when it was going to happen, but I was going to be damn sure I was prepared for it when it did happen, and I was.

When Javen asked me if I could play, I said yes, remember? And when he followed up that question with, "Do you play good?" I was also ready for that question. "Well, I think I play pretty good."

It was the practice that gave me confidence to say that. All that hard work leading up to that yes—that's what made all the difference.

You can't wish your problems away. I couldn't wish and hope to play the piano good enough. I had to put in the work. I had to sweat and stress a little. Nothing was guaranteed, but what mattered was the work—doing the work God gave me to do. And doing it with all my heart.

Hope is not a strategy. But practice is, and a pretty good one at that.

NO SUCH THING AS HOPELESSNESS

Let's talk about the word *hopelessness*.

There is no such thing.

I know you're thinking, *Well, that's easy for him to say. He doesn't know my circumstances. He doesn't know how hard my life is.*

Boo-freaking-hoo.

There is no such thing.

I know it may feel like it sometimes. Overwhelming situations may arise, and circumstances may seem insurmountable, but they're not. The moment God sent his only Son to die in your place because of the sin that invaded the world, hope came alive. Hope for all mankind was attainable. It's right there, and all you have to do is reach out and take it.

But life can throw its weight around, can't it? And after going a few rounds with this beast we call life, we can get bruised and worn.

You're alone.

You're disillusioned.

You've lost your job.

Your heart has been broken.

Someone you trusted has betrayed you.

Your spouse isn't who you thought they were.

These, and so many more, are valid reasons to feel hopeless. It's very tough for you to see your way through the darkness. But when you can't see, you have to trust even more the One who can. After all, what good is faith if you can't deploy it—if you can't use it?

Now, I love the *Rocky* movies and faith. In *Rocky*, the main character, Rocky, had a trainer named Mickey who was gritty as hell and was always pushing him, challenging him, always there for him with pithy wisdom and a show of support. Well, faith is like your own personal Mickey lying on the mat beside you, imploring you to get up for One. More. Round. (Cue Bill Conti's musical theme.)

I only say this because I've been there. Even in the midst of life's successes, I have felt hopeless, scared, and alone. But the greatest lesson I've ever learned was to be still. Sometimes I believe that's all God wants from us—to be still, listen, wait, and then watch as he shows us he is in control of it all. After all, doesn't the Bible tell us in Philippians 4:6, "Do not be anxious about anything"?

Stillness gives perspective. And in my life, the hopeless-feeling times were the times when I most needed to gain a new perspective. In stillness, we can see the future more clearly while adjusting the rearview mirror to gain wisdom from the past.

Have you ever asked what it means to pursue stillness in our hyperconnected, loud, screaming, crazy world? Seems impossible, even as I sit here checking my social media feeds and email. The word *stillness* points to the absence of movement or sound. I don't know about you, but not moving and being in a place where sound doesn't exist is quite literally impossible.

Or is it?

I'm the one who makes the decisions about what I watch and how often. I'm the one plugging into every device known to mankind. I'm the one with the hectic schedule that keeps me in constant motion. So, believe me when I say I know that trying to carve out time to be still and listen and pray is incredibly challenging. I'm not trying to burden you—or me, for that matter!—with an impossible task.

But what I've found is that sometimes I have to be very intentional in doing the things that matter most. For example, I am, or at least try to be, intentional about being present in the lives of my children. Same goes for time away with my wife. Those relationships represent my top priorities.

In the same way, I try to be intentional about getting away from the pace and noise of the world. I try to find little pockets of time when I can get quiet before God and open my heart to him.

And here's what I've found: You don't have to quit your job and become a religious mystic to pursue stillness, to be a person who listens to God. I believe you and I can do that in small pockets of time. I believe sometimes all it takes is a few moments of quiet prayer before bed or the solitude of a quiet house in the morning. It doesn't matter when and for how long. I believe what matters most is that you and I seize the small moments daily.

I know a guy who gets his quiet in during his morning shower. Others use their commute time. And others use their time on a stationary bike. The point is, if you desire perspective in your life—the kind of perspective you need to help you see all the hope spread out before you—then it's important to make time to get quiet, get still, and see the world through heaven's eyes.

A GOOD SADNESS

This reality of success looks fantastic from the outside, from the perspective of an observer. But I've lost track of the times I've thought to myself how this destination we like to call success has turned out to be more than I bargained for. Of course, I'm grateful for the blessings God has given to me and my family. But those blessings also required sacrifice. You never sit and think of the long months, even years, of loneliness you must endure. It's sobering to look at the difference between your dreams and your current reality.

Sometimes I feel a bit of sadness when I look back on my life.

Not the kind of sadness that cripples us or causes us to feel defeated, but the kind of sadness that comes with the bumps and bruises along the way. Things like missing out on family moments, moving from home and missing time with our mom and dad—all the things that life requires from us.

Inevitably, the sacrifices we make catch up to us and leave us sad.

It's the kind of sadness that lets me keep heartstrings attached to the things I love. It's the kind of sadness that accompanies nostalgia. I look at the moments like this: If I'm not sad about something, like not being able to visit home as often as I wanted to, then how much does it really mean to me? If it meant nothing to me, would I feel anything about it at all? Of course not.

I'm not trying to be your shrink. I know this feels like Psych 101, but hang with me here. This kind of sadness doesn't have to leave you in despair. Rather, it's the kind that comes along with taking a job overseas, going to college, missing out on a family reunion because of commitments, or losing loved ones.

See? Sadness doesn't have to be negative. It can be beautifully melancholy. It can be good and appropriate when it means the loss of something meaningful.

It can remind, encourage, and inspire.

Give yourself permission to be sad about the things that matter. You can use these sad moments as stepping-stones to fill in the cracks on your broken road to contentment. Sadness doesn't have to cripple you. It can give you strength.

That's what it does for me.

It reminds me of the sacrifices made at times when I knew without a shadow of a doubt that God had opened a door for me. And I was ready, by his grace, for that opened door. And even though I've experienced this special kind of good sadness along the way, I can say that my soul feels satisfied. And not just because I've achieved my goals as a musician. I'm satisfied because I've learned to be still and rest in God's grace for me. He has always looked out for me, even when I wasn't thinking about him. That's a humbling reminder to thank him for the good sadness. In a weird way, the sadness keeps me grounded.

I've learned that this kind of contentment comes as a result of the strength gained during times of hopelessness. The trick is to not lose sight of that truth. Remember, each moment you go through in life is another stone cemented into the foundation of the life God is leading you to. And our sad moments are part of that foundation. They stack up. In fact, they can be used as stepping-stones on the broken road to the life you can be content with.

When I first started looking back on my story, I thought I had nothing much to say—until my wife and my mom told me how selfish I was for not wanting to share. Imagine my mom pulling me by the ear over to my desk, sitting me down and making me type on this computer through all hours of the night. No, that didn't really happen. But it felt like that at the time.

Not really.

But seriously, it wasn't until I went back in time—sitting with old memories, revisiting the past—that I realized how many God moments have defined my life. I realized how God's grace led me down the path of hope. Little nuggets all along the road— nuggets of hope. If we could grab coffee and chat about life, I'd tell you this one thing: Never give up on hope. It may be elusive, but it's there. The road may be tough, the way narrow, the pain unbearable. But just keep walking.

Chapter 15

SHOTGUN ANGELS

Yet this I call to mind
and therefore I have hope.

THE TEACHER, LAMENTATIONS 3:21

The desire to write this book rose up in me a few years ago. I thought that maybe my story could connect or inspire other people to stay the course and pursue their dreams and never give up hope. I suppose I thought this because I love hearing stories about how people have overcome obstacles in life and find beauty after everything has turned to ashes.

You'll remember I told you the story about how my dad loaded a shotgun and set it by the door when he took me away from Mom. I was eight, and they had just separated and divorced. The bitter taste of separation was no doubt still on my dad's lips when he pulled that stunt.

It's a moment I'll never forget. I don't blame Dad for that, though it scared the living daylights out of me. But you know, it also reminded me of the crazy love my dad had for me. That may sound twisted, but when I think back on that occasion, I can in some ways relate to a love that says, "There's no way you're taking my kid away from me." It was a misguided action, but I believe it stemmed from love. In fact, all of it did. He loved my mom too, and his actions, although poorly executed, reflected that love. He just didn't know how to process the anger and the hurt he was feeling.

Then I remember my mom picking me up from summer church camp on two dollars of gas and a couple of flat tires—driving 186 miles round trip on nothing but angel's wings. It's another story that demonstrates crazy love for me, as well as a strong Christian faith that defined and still defines my mom's very existence. Nothing shakes her. She cares not at all about what the world says, but only about what God says. She lives by that faith, and I paid attention.

It's the same faith I now claim as my own. Not because I inherited it from Mom or somehow acquired it from my dad. It's a faith that proved itself to me over and over again, even when I walked away from it and lived for myself.

I've come a long way from those days of living for myself, barreling down the shotgun road of party madness and destruction. And it's all because of God's grace that I've endured and made it to this place. Now I have my own family. I'm teaching my own kids how to play by ear. I'm loving my wife with my own crazy love and deep faith. I don't always get it right (she would definitely tell you that!), but I'm doing the best I can—all the while pursuing a life of music that was instilled in me by my dad, my mom, and my pappaw. This is my story. This is my life.

YOUR SHOTGUN ANGELS

But what about everybody else?

What about this world of insanity in which we live?

You know, I like to begin our shows by inviting the audience into our little party. We like to invite them to shove off to the side all the bullcrap that's going on in the world today. At our concerts we like to think of the world of our audience as being a world in which there are no divisions; we're all for one and one for all. And then we have a good time and rock the joint.

Can I say that as a country artist? I love it; the guys love it;

and it never gets old. We love bringing folks together and escaping for an hour and a half.

I think in our world today we forget about each other's shotgun angels. We forget about the stories that shape people, both for the good and for the not-so-good. We forget that behind the perfect-looking veneer we see on social media, television, and the internet, behind the professional voices we hear on talk radio, we're all special people with unique stories that have shaped us into who we are.

What if we took one minute at the start of each day to remember that every person is special, every person possesses dignity, every person matters? As C. S. Lewis put it, "There are no *ordinary* people. You have never talked to a mere mortal."[1]

What if before we log on, charge up, or tune in, we take a moment to remember the moments that have made us who we are—and also to remember that everyone has those moments. The schoolteacher? She has those moments. The older gentleman at Home Depot? He has those moments. That picture-perfect person on social media? They're not an avatar; they're a human being, and they have feelings. They have shotgun angel moments that define them. And they deserve our respect, our patience, and our tolerance.

I guess what I'm saying is let's work harder to live a life in which we can know what it means to agree to disagree. That doesn't mean we dismiss people or demean them if they hold a different perspective than we do. It's so easy to do, and we've all done it.

It does mean we listen to see if there's some middle ground where we can discuss things, where we can stop the shouting and live in relative peace and harmony in a world that feels like it's going to hell a million miles a minute. Most of us can find some kind of common ground if we really try.

Let's try to think about the very real dangers every person around us faces, and the shotgun angels that have protected them along the road. Let's try to think about the stories of every individual that have led to where they are and who they are. Maybe if we can live with that perspective, we'll start treating people differently, and we'll get back to being the country I know and love—the one where people stand together, fight for each other, and stand on the hoods of their cars waving American flags with a pint of beer in their hands. The hatred and divisiveness we witness today are destroying the fabric of who we are. We're being torn apart from the inside out. Love, patience, kindness, and just plain old human decency seem to have gone the way of the dinosaur. Okay, well, maybe I got a little carried away on that bit about the beer and the flag, but you get the idea.

We could all do with some human kindness.

I'M RIDING SHOTGUN

"I got shotgun!"

Remember saying that when you were in high school—riding along in the passenger seat, the "other" front seat that was the seat of freedom? No backseat vision impairment. You could see it all. You were the copilot. The coolest was riding along with an older friend when you couldn't drive. Of course, when I'm saying "you," I'm meaning "me."

Riding shotgun? Man, that was me riding with the driver, and thus I was also as cool as the driver. Now, I'm not so sure I had too many people who were excited to ride shotgun in the old I-Mark. But hey, I'm proud of that car.

Who doesn't love to ride shotgun? We all love the kind of shotgun riding in which someone wants nothing but the best for you and is watching out for you. They've got your back.

Think about it like this. We've all got shotgun angels—angels riding shotgun with us as we live this life. Each instance in my life that challenged me? Scared me? Wounded me? I can look back and see my shotgun angels. God was putting them to work. When I was crushed by the divorce of my parents? Shotgun angels—Pappaw took over in my life and became the presence I needed and wanted. He was there for me with his time, with his wisdom, with his art, with his passions.

And what was it that day at the conference that led me down to the stage to talk to Javen? What was it that moved in and out of our conversation? Remember, Javen said he just got a "sense" about me. And Danny said the same thing—there was something inside me that he wanted to uncover. I like to think there were shotgun angels watching over me, whispering into Javen's heart and Danny's heart. I like to think that God was moving all over that conversation and directing it in order to carry out his purposes for me.

My mom lives every day with no doubt that Jesus works in our daily lives. Some people may think that God doesn't care about our silly prayers—the kind of prayers we pray when we're tired or frustrated at work, the times when we're at our wits' end with our spouse (not saying that ever happens to me—love you, babe!), or the times when we didn't get the promotion we thought was coming our way. But God does care about all our prayers, because he cares about us—every single, imperfect one of us.

If you don't think you have shotgun angels riding shotgun in your life, then let me lay this short passage on you from the Old Testament book of Lamentations.

> Yet this I call to mind
> > and therefore **I have hope**:
>
> **Because of the LORD's great love we are not**
> **consumed,**
> > **for his compassions never fail.**
>
> They are new every morning;
> > great is your faithfulness.
>
> I say to myself, "The LORD is my portion;
> > therefore I will wait for him."
>
> **The LORD is good to those whose hope is in him**,
> > to the one who seeks him;
>
> **it is good to wait quietly** [See, stillness is good!]
> > for the salvation of the Lord.
>
> It is good for a man to bear the yoke [Not totally sure
> > what this means, but I like the sound of it! Maybe it
> > means it's sometimes good to endure hard times.]
> > > while he is young
>
> Let him sit alone in silence,
> > for the Lord has laid it on him.
>
> Let him bury his face in the dust—
> > **there may yet be hope**.
>
> Let him offer his cheek to one who would strike him
> > [Whoa! Seems radical in this day and age!]
> > > and let him be filled with disgrace.
>
> For no one is cast off
> > by the Lord forever.

Though he brings grief, he will show compassion,
so great is his unfailing love.
For he does not willingly bring affliction
or grief to anyone [Yes, good to know!].

Lamentations 3:21–33, emphasis added

I know some people don't like the idea of God being a copilot. Remember those old "God is my copilot" stickers you'd see on bumpers back in the 1980s? If you weren't around in the '80s, we still had bumper stickers back then in the Stone Age. And you know, I don't think the idea of God as copilot is too offensive. I totally get that in the hierarchy of life, God is number one. He's running the show.

But the point the bumper sticker was trying to communicate was that, "Hey, I'm in this life *with God.*" Not only that, I don't really like the visual of him as the pilot, because that would mean he was making me go everywhere. Instead the choice is ours. But he is there, right beside us. Even on the wrong turns.

He's my navigator. I'm listening to him. He's the one I lean on when I need help. He's my shotgun angel. This passage in Lamentations reminds me of this fact.

His compassions toward me and for me are new every morning. Every. Single. Morning.

His mercy never fails.

He is faithful.

He loves me.

And it's good for me to hope in him.

It's good for me to wait, to listen, to be still before the Lord.

I'm not sure what your view of God is. And I don't know how hopeful your heart is, but I do know that if you are searching for a light in this dark and messed-up world, then having God riding shotgun is a great place to start. All you have to do is invite him along on the ride. And having him to lean on, to yell at, to cry to, will comfort you for sure. But it also gives you hope beyond measure. I would ask you this: *What do you have to lose?*

Even if you've never been exposed to religion or to Christianity, what would it hurt to try something new? What if I told you it's a much easier way to navigate the waters of this thing called life? Now I know it may be oversimplifying things a bit, but if someone told me there was an easier way to get my teeth cleaned than going to the dentist, I would jump at the chance!

The evidence of having hope is not about achieving some measure of success; the evidence of having hope is about receiving the strength to get through the next day, through the next chapter of your life. I had hope in the bank plenty of times, and nothing to show for it. You can't measure your hope by success. You measure it by your willingness to keep moving forward.

MY ULTIMATE HOPE

*There is nothing noble in being superior
to some other man. The true nobility is in
being superior to your previous self.*

W. L. SHELDON

Now listen, I didn't write this book to suggest for one second that I've got everything figured out. Trust me, I'm still a work in progress. I shared with you at the beginning that I had many reservations about writing a book. At the end of the day, I wanted to share my ride with you so you could see someone who was real, someone like you—someone who has made mistakes, who continues to make mistakes, who sometimes learned from them (and sometimes not) and has done the very best he could with whatever life put on his plate.

The problem is, life does not come neatly wrapped in a bow. It's messy. It's hard. What really blows is there is no handbook. I'd give anything to read a chapter about "Not Drinking Too Much in Vegas, Thus Gambling Too Much Money Away." I could've used its wise counsel.

Or how about "How to Not Suck at Juggling Kids and Career"? A lot of us would probably have that chapter highlighted, with abundant notes in the margins.

My wife could probably fill this book with things I still need to work on personally, but the point is, I'm trying. I believe that's all anyone can ever ask or expect from us. The trying, the doing. The constant pursuit of trying to be the best you can be.

My only thing is, don't do it alone. We're not made to!

If we were capable of handling all this crap alone, we'd have no need for friends, for Oprah, or for . . . a Savior. God doesn't call us to perfection. He simply calls us to be open and honest enough with ourselves to say, "I'm screwed up. I need help, and I need all the grace I can get because sometimes it feels like I'm never going to get it right."

To me, that's the ultimate hope. Knowing there's someone sitting on the throne of heaven always ready to hear me, fight for me, and wrap his arms back around me—even when I've strayed from him as far as I could go.

My dear friend Mark Lowry used to say, "You know why God's mercies are new every day? Because we wear them out all day long!" I've sure felt like that before, haven't you? Like there was no way in the world that grace could cover up all the mistakes and wrongs I've done? I've got news for you—it does.

You are covered.

So, what's today going to be like for you? Are you going to be courageous? Are you going to push yourself to take chances, to risk everything you have for something you love? Or will you fall back on the long list of reasons you've compiled over the years of why you shouldn't?

I could never do that.

That's someone else's job.

I'm just an amateur.

What if I fall flat on my face?

And on and on it goes.

That list is extensive, I'm sure. I had a list. We all do. But long ago, in a car on the way to Lee University, to the house of a guy I barely knew in Cleveland, Tennessee, I tore up my list. I shredded it.

Tear yours up.

Set fire to it if you have to.

Get moving.

Go out and pursue your dreams with the determination that nothing will stop you. Will it all be perfect? Most likely not. But if you work hard and are prepared for the next opportunity you have, you can be brave and take the leap. There will undoubtedly be setbacks, times when you're frustrated and don't know what to do. But keep your eyes and your heart open, and I promise you this . . .

Hope will find you.

ACKNOWLEDGMENTS

First of all, I want to thank my publishing team at Zondervan for presenting me with this wonderful opportunity. I have discovered a new love of writing, and I owe that to them. Their support throughout this entire process has been second to none.

Kathy Olen, you've always been a such huge supporter of all things "Jay DeMarcus." I cannot thank you enough for your belief in me. I could never have done this without you.

Tim Willard, thank you for your patience on this journey. I'm sure writing with a complete novice has had its challenges, but I'm so proud of what we've done together—and even more proud to call you my friend.

To all the people in this book, and out of it, whom I did not have the space or time to mention—you know who you are. Thank you, and God bless you for the little things—things you may not even know about—that you did to affect me on this journey. I love to collect moments, and I have so many millions that I hold dear to my heart, that have piled up over the years. When I look back on the moments with friends and people I love and hold dear, I realize that I am a very rich man who is blessed more than I ever deserved.

To my mother—a big part of this book is about the woman you are, and how your faith helped shaped me from an early age. Thank you for being a rock and such a bright beacon of hope for me to see the reflection of Christ in you. I love you dearly. Dad, I love you. You passed on your passion of music. You pushed me to be better at my craft and instilled in me a desire to do everything I attempt to the very best of my ability. My sister, Tiffany, who put up with the loud drums and guitars—and a brother completely obsessed with music who probably drove her crazy from time to time—always believed in me, defended me, encouraged me, and stood behind me through everything, both the good and the bad.

My brothers Gary and Joe Don. None of this happens without what we've built and bled for together. You are two of the most remarkably talented people I know. I love you both dearly, and I thank God every day that our "broken roads" came together.

My heavenly Father—you are the cause of it all. You have allowed me the privilege to live this life, look back on it, and see your hand in *all* of it. I know I haven't always chosen my paths wisely, but with every twist and turn you've been there with your arms wide open, loving me, extending unmerited grace to me, and calling me yours. For that I am eternally astounded and forever grateful.

NOTES

CHAPTER 4: All That and a Sack of Potatoes

1. "Hope," Oxford Dictionaries, https://en.oxforddictionaries .com/definition/hope.

CHAPTER 6: More Wild Turns

1. See Isaiah 55:8.
2. Psalm 103:12.

CHAPTER 9: My Downward Spiral

1. Quoted in Andrew Motion, *Keats: A Biography* (Chicago: University of Chicago Press, 1997), 257.

CHAPTER 10: Losing My Way

1. C. S. Lewis, *The Problem of Pain* (San Francisco: HarperOne, 2015), 92.
2. Philip Yancey, *Disappointment with God: Three Questions No One Asks Aloud*, 25th anniv. ed. (1988: repr., Zondervan, 2015), 263, italics original.
3. See 1 Peter 5:7.

CHAPTER 11: Fiddle and Steel

1. See Brittany Fietsam, Minsu Kim, and Lejla Pracic, "Honky Tonk," Country Music Project, http://sites.dwrl.utexas.edu/ countrymusic/the-history/honky-tonk.

CHAPTER 13: Beautiful Winds the Broken Road

1. Mark 10:18.
2. 1 Peter 1:15.
3. The song was written by Marcus Hummon, Jeff Hanna, and Bobby Boyd.
4. Lewis Hyde, *The Gift: Creativity and the Artist in the Modern World*, 25th anniv. ed. (New York: Vintage, 2007), 188–89, italics original.

CHAPTER 14: Eternal Sadness of a Satisfied Soul

1. Matthew 14:22–33.

CHAPTER 15: Shotgun Angels

1. C. S. Lewis, *The Weight of Glory* (1949: repr., San Francisco: HarperSanFrancisco, 2001), 46, italics original.